RESIDENTIAL SCHOOL

A HOME AWAY FROM HOME

RAJENDRA PRASAD DOBHAL

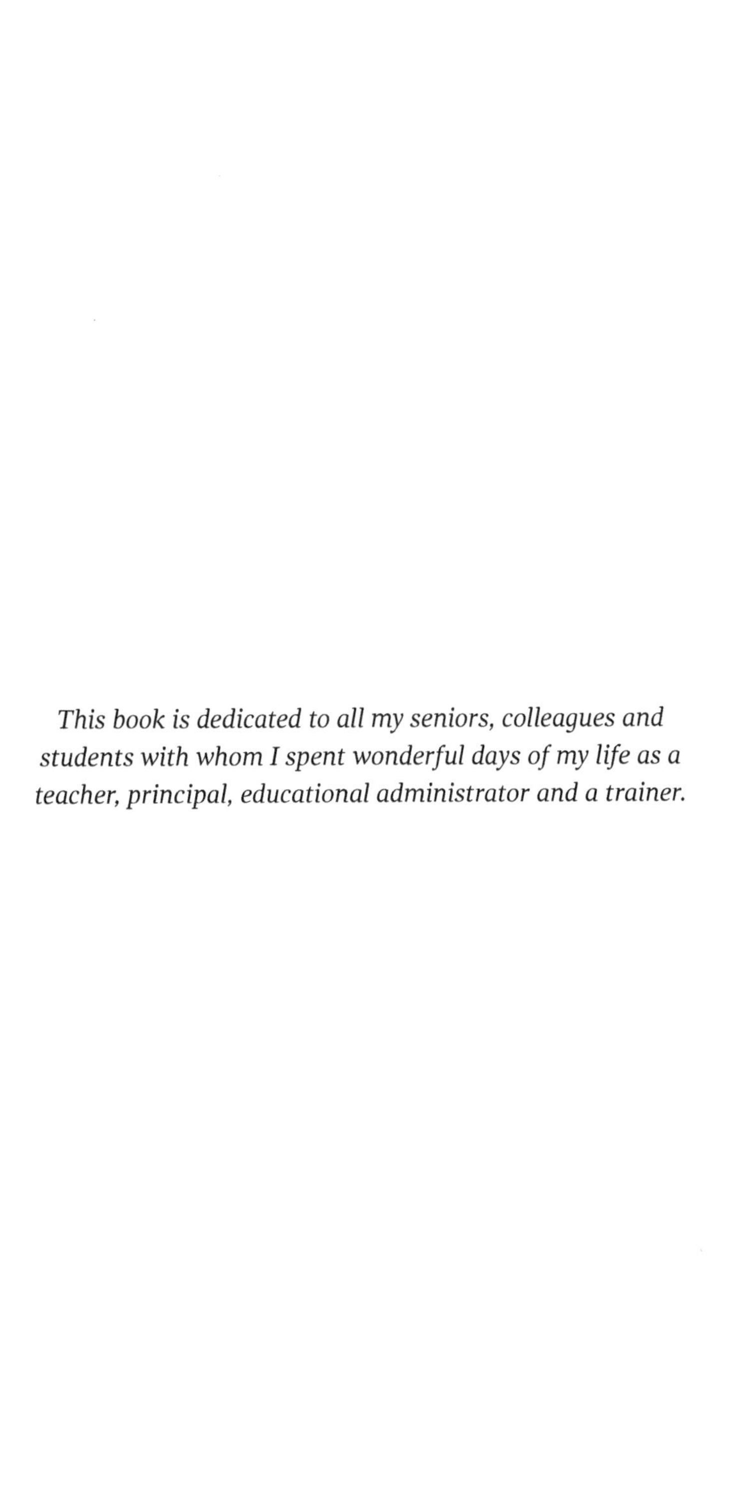

This book is dedicated to all my seniors, colleagues and students with whom I spent wonderful days of my life as a teacher, principal, educational administrator and a trainer.

Contents

Contents

vi

Preface

After having served for about forty long years in exclusively residential schools both private and govt. an idea of jotting down my vast and varied experiences struck in my mind. I started recollecting all those sweet and sour memories of my stint as a teacher, principal, educational administrator and trainer. This book is the outcome of all that.

A residential school provides the best platform to accomplish the ultimate aim of education i.e. 'Holistic Personality Development'. These schools are known for their healthy traditions, systems, values, parental care, scholastic and co-scholastic activities. . Therefore, a residential school is not only a center of excellence but ' A Home Away From Home'. I have seen, felt and experienced this in every school that I served. The principal, teachers and students have such a strong bonding that they feel at home. May be the parents are not there but the foster parent the principal, teachers and all others are more caring, affectionate and attentive. There are guides, coaches and mentors. There are friends, brothers and sisters. The activities that the children undertake at home ieTuition, coaching, games, sports and all others are available in school itself. The homely and friendly environment, personal attention, disciplined lifestyle.ie, gainfully busy routine are the systems that convert school into a home and therefore, it is a ' Home Away From Home'.

A Residential School is always abuzz with one or the other activities. The bubbling enthusiasm of the teachers and taught, hustle and bustle in and around, togetherness, sense of belongingness, Strong disciplinary system, regulatory environment, diginity of labour, cultivation of good habits and values, character building, quality formal and moral education and many other features make it a school and home as well. Live and Learn together is the basic philosophy of a Residential School. All teachers and students are groomed in such a way that they are able to articulate the basic philosophy of Excellence. This is to be reinforced again and again through various platforms.

CHAPTER I

Idea, Concept and the System

"Education is the manifestation of perfection already in man
Education is the process of HRD which helps to achieve better and higher quality of life."

The idea of Residential Education perhaps figured in the mind of great saints, the GURUS who might have thought that providing better education and imbibing good values is possible only out of home. The love, affection and comforts at home would rather create hindrances in getting education. Thus the Idea of Residential Education is the product of highly intellectual minds. These prudent people lived lonely lives in forests and Hills. They were always busy in devotion and meditation, far from the world of other human beings. The then Kings and even the Devtas used to visit them, sought blessings and guidance. All of them discussed their worries of Good Education of their siblings because of the absence of good teachers. Although these great Gurus were detached from the worldly affairs but seriously concerned about the welfare of the society. They were clear in their thoughts that education is the best tool to transform humans.

This was the time when the IDEA of providing Residential Education might have appeared in their minds. They were in fact thinking to give a practical shape to this idea and ultimately they succeeded. From this noble thought the CONCEPT of Residential Education cropped.

Even the Gods and Demons had to leave their respective homes and all comforts to seek education. For a certain period they went to Ashrams of eminent saints, hermits and Gurus. All of us have heard about great Vrihaspati and Shukrachary. They sacrificed their luxuries and lived a very simple and tough life in Ashrams. Apart from value based religous education they were taught fighting skills, music, dance and other arts.

The great Gurus were of the firm opinion that knowledge wealth is above all wealths,

वद्यिा धनम सर्वधनम प्रधानम and also स्वदेशे पूज्यते राजा वद्विान सर्वत्र पूज्यतो a king is worshipped in his country but a scholar is worshipped everywhere.

The idea of great Rishis and Gurus was conceptualized and The system of Residential Educational centres came into being. Initially the Asrams of great gurus began to provide education but to elite ones only. These Asrams gradually became so popular that all great kings sent their princes to them. Our epics Ramayana, Mahabharata and others are full of the description of all this. This was the only Best System of Education in those ages. The Asrams became the centres of Excellence. The deciples very seriously learnt religion, culture, fighting skills and obeyed and respected their gurus.

With the passage of time the Gurukuls came into being where the eminent scholars provided quality residential education. Nalanda and Taxsila were well known Gurukuls which later on became Universities where no stone was unturned to shape the personality of the deciples. Quality Education was provided to the students hailing from all over the country as well as the neighboring countries. Nalanda and Taxila are the best examples of these centres of excellence where the great scholars Chanakya, Panini, Jeevaka, Atisha taught and students like Chandra Gupta, Harshvardhan, Aryabhatta and Nagarjuna were produced.

This System of Wholesome Residential Education was appreciated all over the world and gradually many Institutes of repute were set up. In modern times the Church and Christian Missionaries played a very important role in setting up the residential schools particularly in America, Europe and India. Initially these schools were established to impart education to the officers and cadres of the Colonizers so they are intact with their Religion and Culture on the foreign land where they ruled . Gradually the wards of affluent sections were also permitted to join.

Thus the system of Residential Education emerged as one of the best and most reliable systems to provide quality education in the world.

Residential school is a progressive forward looking concept. It has been widely accepted all over and with a result many schools came into being. Earnest efforts are made by all functionaries to create a homely environment and therefore the school becomes a home away from home. The school strives hard for the sustainable future through resilience, innovation and excellence.

CHAPTER II

Residential School System

"सतं की वह कौन सी भकि्षा थी,
सतं द्वारा दी जान ेवाली शकि्षा थी।
गुरुकुल शकि्षा का एक अच्छा नविास ह,ै
उस शकि्षा की हम ेफरि तलाश ह"ै

आदर्श सनि्हा"

A System is formed by a group of people having common ideologies for a particular scheme based on certain procedures, regulations and principles. It is the combination of many subsystems which are related with each other. They function together to accomplish prescribed vision and Mission. Although the Residential School System has its Genesis centuries old, the growing trend took place from the 19th century. A number of Residential Schools came into being in Europe and America. The Britishers set up a good number of such schools in India and elsewhere. In the beginning of 20th century The Residential School System gathered a fast momentum and a number of Boarding schools became so popular that gettimg admission in these schools was rather very tough.Thus a new System of Schools came to be known as Residential School System.

Any system consists of several other subsystems. These systems play a pivotal role in the overall functioning of The main system. The Residential Schools System also consists of a number of SubSystems

surrounding it. All these subsystems are interrelated and interdependent. They function together to realize the objectives of the System. All these subsystems endeavor to educate children on the basis of their basic philosophy, traditions and ideals. The residential school is known for the atmosphere of freedom as well as responsibility. The system creates a home like relationship and environment where the children live and learn together and adapt to it. **Principals and teachers become the loco parents and leave no stone unturned to nurture the young minds.** The students attain a reasonable level of competence and excel in life. They get ample opportunities for self development, shaping their personalities in order to become responsible citizens and excellent professionals. **Competence, commitment, culture and responsibility are the most dominating features.**

Though the learners hail from different backgrounds, experiences, preferences, customs and traditions yet they unitedly learn and develop themselves. The system of Residential School provides equal opportunities to grow and develop. The healthy traditions of these schools, homely environment and teachers dedication not only train the students to excel in academics but also in all spheres of life. **Self confidence, self reliance, team spirit, leadership development, dignity of labour are some of the most dominating features of Residential School. The** bubbling enthusiasm of students make them vibrant and strong. A variety of futuristic programs of these schools contributed to the popularity and rapid growth of these schools. Every school proves to be a gateway to success.

Residential School System consists of several other related systems for smooth sailing. These subsystems function together to accomplish a common objective i.e.

to provide Quality Education for Wholesome personality development. These are interrelated and interdependent. **Some of the subsystems are Residential System, House System, Mess System, Safety and Security System, supervised study system, academic management system, finance system, HRD System, CCA System etc.** Every residential school selects a team of talented professionals to achieve it's vision and mission. Their unwavering dedication and commitment to transform the young lives is always praise worthy. Apart from strong academics, value addition is a very important component of every residential school. A very high level of engagement of teachers and taught with resonance is the key to success of every residential school. **The state of art infrastructure, excellent physical facilities, very strong support system, result driven scholastic and co-scholastic activities, preventive and corrective disciplinary provisions , healthy traditions and well settled alumni make the system a robust one.** The schools set new standards, set the pace and thus become the leaders in education. The Residential School always has a very strong Alumni network which becomes the strength of the school.

Over the time residential education has become the need of the hour. Ever since globalization emerged, the number of working parents has tremendously increased. The working parents look for a residential school in order to provide good education and better well being of their wards, the residential schools attract a large number of parents and young minds. These schools proved to be a Renaissance in education fostering an environment congenial and conducive to quality learning having no scope for dogmatic teaching learning Styles. The system of a residential school connects the students with various experiences and opportunities to help them to succeed in life. It is the most appealing system where the personalities are shaped in such a **passion that children feel at home and therefore, the school is known as Home Away from Home.**

Mandatory participation in school activities develops self confidence and motivates them to come forward and show their Worth. Child becomes adventurous and bold. Adventure activities are the integral part of every Residential School. The students become adventure junkies.

The meaning of education in a Residential School is more than that of accumulation of knowledge. The school sets healthy traditions, strives for the best in every sphere and phenomenal transformation of personalities. It connects the learners to new experiences and opportunities. Huge and scenic campus, state of art facilities, stress on physical and mental well being, supportive **and conducive learning environment make a Resident School a top notch one, a premier Institution and thus becomes most appealing.**

Residential Schools not only educate the minds but the hearts as well. Students equally acquire IQ as well as EQ. They become both Head Smart as well as Heart Smart. Schools known for empowered minds and energized souls. The stimulating and challenging environment of the school encourages creativity and innovations. **Dr. Radhakrishnan had very aptly differentiated between the Station Master and a School Master. A Station Master Minds the Trains and a School Master trains the minds.**

Residential school is unparalleled in the quality of talents. Some of the schools are unmatched and unbeatable in every field of functioning. These schools not only educate but also regulate and empower. Therefore, the residential schools are at the helm and forefront of quality education. They have changed the narratives of school education. **The students are tuned in such a manner that they get prepared for 21st century employability so that they can give back to society whatever they received.**

CHAPTER III

Residential Culture

"Education is a man making process. Education is not preparation for life. Education is life itself.
John Dewey"

The word culture can briefly be defined as a combination of certain beliefs, faiths , customs and traditions of a community. In accordance with this definition School is also a Community having a common culture. The school has its own culture consisting of the healthy traditions set by it. The entire school community carries these tradtions further through its various systems. This culture is the way of life of all inmates. The school earns name and fame because of this culture. **In respect of a Residential School efforts are made to create, protect and preserve this culture.**

Residential culture is somehow different from a normal school culture. Every school has its own culture, its systems, academic standard, discipline status and value system. In a residential school The most important part of this culture is the homely environment that the school strives to create. The school endeavors to set such customs, traditions, values and beliefs that become examples for others. The children are not with their parents, the teachers are their loco parents. Because of its healthy traditions the school not only grows but develops and becomes a home for the inmates.

Components of Residential Culture.

Residential Culture comprises several prescribed and not prescribed components. These components all together form the culture of the school which plays a dominating role in the success of the school.

House culture.

Soon after their admission the students are are allotted a house functioning under the leadership of a House Master. School Has House System which provides homely environment to the students. The customs, traditions, discipline, relationship of the house leaves an indelible impact on students. Their unity, mutual understanding, love and affection for each other, respect for elders, sense of discipline, cultivation of good habits, and moral values are the significant contributors to form this culture. Thus an Effective House System is a vital component of Residential Culture.

Congenial and conducive Environment.

Healthy school culture is the outcome of a peaceful and congenial environment in and around the school. Its academic standard, teaching learning strategies, excellent results in both scholastic and co scholastic activities, **safe and secured climate make the school a loveable and liveable entity. This environment of the school is everlasting and hence an important part of the Residential Culture.**

Mess Culture.

Mess is an integral part of Residential Culture. **It is always said that any mess in a Residential School is through mess.** It can be a major source of indiscipline and disturbance. If the quality of meals served is not up to the satisfaction of students they may indulge in any act of indiscipline. Moreover, the students are made to learn table manners, healthy eating habits and self help/service attitude.

Programs for Personality development, values and Attitude.

Residential School provides the best opportunities for holistic personality development. The children are groomed, shaped and moulded in such a passion that they develop all personality traits. They become physically fit, mentally alert and emotionally sound. The culture of school clearly reflects in their outer as well as inner personality. The way they act, think, behave and communicate is praise worthy. In the institutional planning of the school Several programs for personality development are planned and organised from time to time. **Students are taught to change adversities into opportunities.**

Value based education is one of the important features of Residential Culture. It is often said that values can not be taught but ought to be caught. Values filter downwards from the elders to the youngsters. Residential School is also a home for the students, hence inculcation of good values is the responsibility of the principal and teachers.

The students hail from varied backgrounds, faiths and beliefs. Therefore, there may be certain attitudinal problems. The school's teaching learning systems, traditions and overall culture together bring a desirable attitudinal change. They become positive to self and others. This positiveness helps them throughout their life. Positive attitude decides their altitude and gratitude.

"Attitude is a little thing that makes a big difference."
Winston Churchill.

Self Development.

The culture of a Residential School is such that there are ample opportunities for self-development. The children are taught that Self help and self service is the best help. Their dependence is on themselves. Students take care of their belongings their cleanliness, health and hygiene, studies and personality. The students are groomed in such an environment that their Self Esteem automatically becomes high. Their way of viewing themselves transforms tremendously. They don't bother what others think about themselves but their main concern is what they think about themselves. **You can not believe in God unless you believe in self.**

Residential Culture promotes WE feelings rather than I feelings. With these collective feelings The students are always bubbling with enthusiasm and positivity. There is neither time nor the occasions when the students are surrounded with negative thoughts. **They are given to understand that nothing in this world can trouble as much as the negative thoughts..**

Relationship.

One of the most important requirements for the creation of Residential Culture is the building good relations. The students are so closely attached with each other and teachers that the relations like friendship, guardian, mentor, guide automatically develop. Both intra and interpersonal relationships are always helpful in building residential culture. Good relations in the system lead to mutual understanding, trust, respect for seniors and elders and obedience.

Belongingness.

Development of the feelings of ownership is another component of Residential Culture. As already discussed,

Residential School is a Home Away From Home, students are there 24x 7 hrs. They own the system and belong to it.. They become so grateful that they never criticise the system nor allow anbodyelse to do so. They become the members of the school family and always love to come back to their Alma mater on several occasions

Discipline.

Discipline lays the foundation of success. Though inculcating the sense of discipline is the responsibility of every school, in a Residential School where the children are to be looked after and taken care throughout their stay, discipline becomes the first and foremost priority. It is not the hostel, classroom, play field discipline but also the self discipline. It is one of the traditions and values of Residential Schools. Without general and self discipline Residential Schools can not function smoothly and effectively. The products of Residential Schools demonstrate it in every walk of their lives.

Safety and Security.

As discussed earlier the school becomes home only when they feel at home in the school. It is possible when a safe and secured environment exists. Therefore, it is one of the necessities of the residential culture. The parents are often worried about the health and hygiene, their welfare and their adjustment problems. Whenever they visit their wards in the school, safety and security related problems are the main issues brought in their knowledge. Therefore, it is an important component of Residential Culture.

Time Management.

The schedule of a residential school is often very hectic. The students need to be kept gainfully busy every time. Managing time is part of the school's culture. There is hardly any time to be wasted. Daily routine of the school is very tight. There is fixed time for morning PT, exercises, games, sports, supervised and self studies. All activities have to be completed within the stipulated time. Children learn the value of time and its management. Hence it is one of the cultures of the school.

Amity, unity and empathy are important features of Residential Culture.

CHAPTER IV

House System; The Backbone of a Residential School

"Hostel life is an effective way of training the students in the art of living and learning together. Imbibes the values of cooperation, coordination, unity, sacrifice, discipline and brotherhood."

It has already been discussed in previous pages that the Residential School System consists of several subsystems. One of these is the House System. It functions as the backbone of the entire school system. For smooth functioning the students are divided in small units known as houses. This is a systematically and scientifically designed system to take proper pastoral care and develop a sense of belongingness in the learners so that they feel at home. An effective house system is instrumental to realize the objectives of the school. Every child is allotted a house at the entry time and remains in the same house till passing out from the school. Even the colleges and universities have a House System. It also exists in day schools but only for activities.

House system plays a vital role in the Residential School. The class room is meant for providing the child necessary academic background, house is for socialization of learners and developing essential qualities which enable him to face life challenges efficiently and avail opportunities confidently. It provides a family environment and several opportunities for personality development. Universal as well as fundamental values are developed in house.

What is a House?

A House is a portion of a building or hostel where a group of students reside under the supervision of a teacher or his/her associate known as House Masters. There can be four to six such houses depending on the strength of the school. These units are known as Dormitories. The house is like a large family where the members reside together under the guardianship of a senior member, respect each other, create an environment of happiness and satisfaction. The children gradually develop a sense of belongingness, associate themselves, respect the seniors, love the juniors, participate in house activities and make every effort to bring laurels to their house in every sphere.

Objectives of the House System.

Every system has a purpose to be formed. And so is the house system. While the system serves as a support system of the school, the objectives are clearly defined for which every house endvours to achieve. Some of the objectives are as follows..

Development of a sense of discipline, belongingness and unity. The students are brought up in a preventive, protective and regulatory environment so that they understand the importance of discipline for their success in life.

Imbibe good values to strengthen moralityand character. Value orientation through value based education is therefore an important objective of the House System.

Prepare a self dependent and self confident child. Though there are the teachers and house masters to take care of, yet the main caretaker is the child himself/herself.

They are trained in such a manner that they develop the ability to help themselves. There is least dependence on others. Self dependent child is always self confident.

Development of Leadership Qualities is another important objective. Although every school aims at preparing future leaders, the Role of Residential School in this particular direction is paramount. Because of the accomplishment of this objective, the Residential Schools have produced great leaders served and serving the country in defence, civil services, management, politics and elsewhere.

Developing zeal for competition and preparing for various competitions. Residential School is known for various intra and inter school competitions. The inter house competitions are organised frequently.. Every huose prepares the children and initiates and encourages their participation. It is compulsory for every child to participate in one or the other competition as per their interest and personal inclination.

Understanding the value of Dignity of Labour. The children are kept gainfully busy after school hours. They are assigned several tasks such as cleaning, gardening, plantation, house maintenance etc to make them understand the dignity of labour.

Self understanding and high self esteem. An Effective House System aims at developing a sense of Self respect amongst the students. The system enables the students to assess themselves.

Besides, promotion of team spirit, patriotism, obedience, citizenship are some other objectives of the House System.

Formation of Houses.

A group of students consists of a House. There can be four to six houses in the school depending on the total enrollment.The number of house members is usually small so that it is easily managed. For residential purposes the house is allotted a dormitory where the entire house is accommodated. There can be Senior house and junior house dormitories. In some of the schools senior and juniors are mixed and in some others they are separated. A house is headed by a House Master followed by one or two deputies, depending on the strength of the House. Every house has a House Prefect or Captain and his one or two Deputies. Every teacher of the school is also associated with one or the other house.

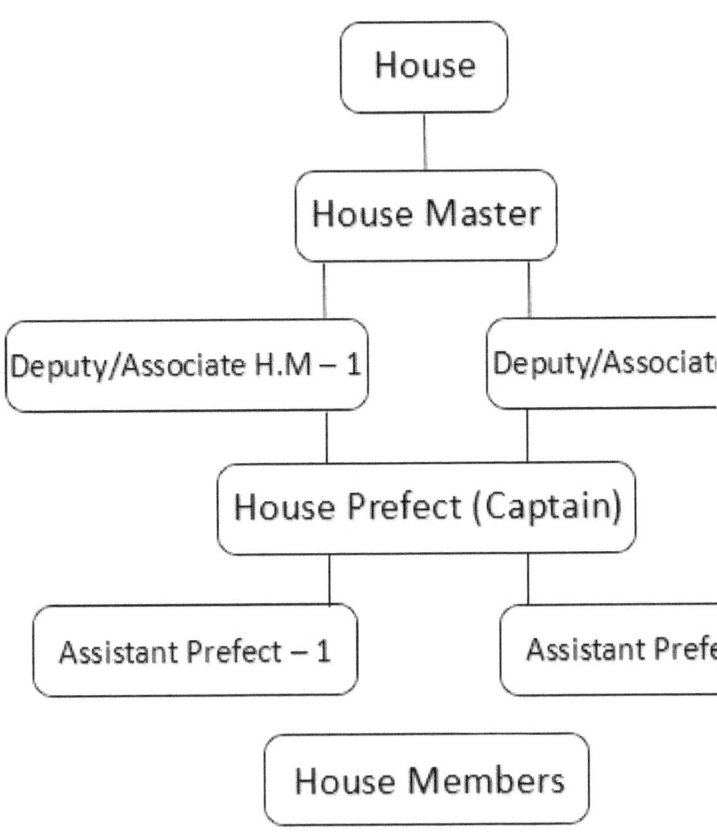

The House System

How does the House System Function?

Every House functions under the supervision and guidance of a House Master and an Associate or Deputy House Master. They are the teachers of the school given additional responsibility. They are compensated in terms of some remuneration or facility. They are generally senior and experienced teachers. All other teachers are also allotted houses for participation, encouragement, motivation of house and smooth functioning .

The Houses are named after

- great patriots like Subhash, Gandhi, Tagore or
- flowers as Rose, Daisy, lotus or
- rivers as Ganga, Kaveri, Jamuna or
- colours like Red, Yellow, Green etc.
- mountains such as Himalaya, Aravali, Everest etc.

Names of houses remain the same for both boys and girls in a co-educational school . Every House has its motto, symbol and colour.

Role and Responsibilities of House Master

House Master has multi-dimensional roles in a Residential School. HM is not only responsible but also accountable for the smooth functioning of the House. The children are very close to the HM. They share all their pleasures and disappointments with the HM. Hence HM is their guardian, guide, mentor, friend and teacher. There are varied roles of HM and with every role a number of responsibilities are attached. These can be described as under...

As a parent

House masters are the House Parents. Their duties and responsibilities are similar to that of parents at home. They help the students in their adjustment and socialization in the new environment. The pastoral care love and affection, taking care of emotional needs, guardianship etc are the parental duties of House Masters.

HM as an Administrator

The House Master has to maintain proper displine in the house. He has to ensure that the students do not indulge in any act of indiscipline in the hostel. All rules and regulations are to be strictly complied with. The safety and security arrangements are perfect. Preventive measures are adopted to ensure safe and secure living in the school. Any loophole is to be reported to the competent authority. The HM takes necessary steps to prevent any sort of ragging, teasing by seniors . Has to deal Health issues seriously. HM has to interact with the parents from time to time. Monitoring of daily routine is also very much within the preview of the HM. Has to ensure that the students strictly follow the routine and turn up timely for their classes, activities, supervised studies, meals and elsewhere. The roll call in the house has to be taken on a regular basis.

HM as an Academician

HMs are teachers also. They have to be in constant touch with the academic progress and achievements of their students. They supervise their self studies in the hostel and provide necessary assistance. Subjects difficulties are discussed with concerned teachers. Being their guardian and teacher, students feel free to come forward with their problems. The parents are also informed and spoken about the academic achievements of their wards from time to time.

HM as a Manager

The House Master has to manage all affairs of the house. Has to ensure proper physical facilitate, cleanliness, health and hygiene, house activities, maximum participation of students, their daily needs etc. The HM has also to supervise the mess system of the school so that quality meals are served to the students.

HM as a Teacher

As already mentioned that House Masters are teachers also. Maybe their academic workload is slightly lower. If need be the HM teaches his/her subject to the students in hostel or takes extra classes. Monitor their academic performance.

HM as a Leader

A leader is one who knows the way, shows the way and goes the way. Knowledge of every sphere of house system, effectively handling all affairs and motivating the students to follow the rightous way are some of the leadership qualities of a HM . Leader leads, guides, motivates, appreciates, encourages, transforms and sets the highest standards. Leader should be a good listner, must give a patient hearing to the students.

HM as a Person

Along with the above, HM is a person, a human being. Has to provide desired love and affection to the students. He is supposed to be a thorough gentleman, humble, submissive, social, concernned and considerate. **Only a better person can be a better professional. As a person the HM makes the students learn through his/her personality traits.**

Thus while playing many roles the HM very efficiently and effectively discharges his responsibilities. A Residential School becomes a Home only when its House System is effective. Running a Residential School is a Herculean task but an effective House System makes its functioning smooth.

The HMs very efficiently and sincerely perform all these duties, work tirelessly and leave an indelible impact on students.

Besides the HM has the following responsibilities.

Conduct House Meetings

House meetings are integral components of Effective House System. Timely meetings of house members encourages the students to come forward with their suggestions for the betterment of the house. They can also apprise the HM with their personal and House problems. The developments in the school, participation in activities, discipline in the house can be discussed and decisions can be taken.

Record keeping

HM is also the record keeper of the house. A number of Registers need to be maintained. Such records help in gathering and giving feedback to the Principal from time to time. Some of these are movement register, medical care register, activities register, performance register, house meeting register, house attendance register etc.

Counselling and Guidance

HM is the guide and a counsellor of students. He/she has to play a proactive role in the adjustment, adaptation and socialization of the students. Their emotional needs must be fulfilled. Teachers can be the best counsellors, most trustworthy. In a Residential School nobody can understand the students better than their teachers.

House Prefects and their Associates

A senior student of the house is appointed as a House Perfect or House Captain by School Administration. These appointments are other than the Head Boy or Head Girl of the school. House perfect is selected on the basis of overall qualities of a member. His royalty, belongingness, leadership qualities, behavior, attitude, personality etc are the attributes that the school administration considers.

Roles and Responsibilities of House Prefects

1.Providing Leadership to the House

The Prefect is the Leader of the house and housemates are the followers. As a leader the perfect leads them in the right direction in every field. He participates in the decision making process for the house with the HM and the Associates.

2.Work as a link between the House Master and house members

They are always in close contact with their fellow friends and are fully aware of the house developments. Their cooperation and coordination is very significant and useful in house functioning

3. Provide feedback to the House Master.

Feedback mechanism is not a complaint mechanism but providing positive feedback. This feedback is very important to the HM because it helps in resolving the problem/situation.

4.Assist the fellow members to prepare for various intra and inter house activities.

The prefects being senior members are capable enough to guide, train and supervise all such preparations. He himself participates in several such activities and encourages others.

5. Maintenance of proper discipline in the House.

The perfect ensures that the house members strictly adhere to the rules and regulations of the school and the House. He/she is the leader of the house and expected to demonstrate all his/her leadership qualities for the name and fame of the house.

6. House maintenance and cleanliness.

The perfect ascertains that the house is properly maintained by the house members. Their beddings are properly made, belongings are placed orderly and the house is neat and clean.

7. Role modelling.

The House Prefect has to be a role model for the members. He sets the examples and others follow. Because of this he/she becomes respectable and honoured. The house captain plays different roles, a member of the group, community and the society. For him/her mutual understanding is an important tool. Must possess the Ability to benefit self from the qualities of others and impress others from self-qualities. At the same time the captain has to demonstrate a desirable behavior and ensure sound moral character and indelible integrity.

8. Creation of a Supportive and Conducive environment in the House.

House perfect is Big Brother for the house mates. He is their friend, guardian and guide. He supports, keeps friendly, helps ever, hurts never. The conducive environment of the house reflects in the school.

Inter House competitions.

House competitions are integral components of Effective house system. These competitions encourage participation, build confidence, develop team spirit, leadership qualities and bring laurels to the house. Competitions are organized both in scholastic as well as co scholastic activities. Records of such competitions are maintained and points are accorded to the winners. The **Champion House or Cock House is declared on the basis of these points every year.**

Master on Duty(MOD).

In every Residential School MOD is the Master of the Day. MOD can be a teacher as well as a House Master. The duties to MOD are assigned on a daily basis. The presence of MOD is required everywhere during the day. Has to be in morning PT, evening games, mess and supervised studies. Has to be on his/her toes throughout the day.

Thus when we say that a Residential School is a Home away from Home, it is the effective House System which contributes the most to creating a homely environment in school.

CHAPTER V

Safety and Security Concerns

"Prevention is Better than Cure."

School becomes home only when the homely atmosphere is there. The children feel safe and secured at home under the protection and guardianship of their parents. A similar environment needs to be created in Residential School also. **Safety First is** of paramount importance in a Residential School. It is in fact one of the important pillars of the school. Providing a safe and secured environment is the prime responsibility of the school. The teachers and all other concerned have to ensure all measures to provide safety cover to the students. The parents have handed over their most valuable asset to the school and therefore, the accountability of the school in this regard can not be compromised at any cost. Often in schools there are the incidents of accidents, electric shocks, drawning, fire, suicides, fights, clashes and many others of such mature posing threat to life. The chances and frequency of occuranc of such incidents is much more in Residential School because the children are there 24× 7 hrs. Therefore, safety and security becomes the top priority.

According to Abraham Maslow Safely is a Physiological need which must be satisfied. Then only All other needs of love, affection, friendship, esteem, belongingness etc will be fulfilled.

Safety means the quality of being safe. The students are safe in the school when their living is comfortable and there is no fear, threat or danger to their lives. The school administration has to view it very seriously and accord top priority to these issues. All other objectives can be accomplished only when the students are safe and secured in a preventive and protective environment.

Security refers to the measures adopted to ensure safety. A wide range of measures are adopted by the school administration to provide security cover to the staff and students. This is a very sensitive area of the school hence needs to be handled with care. Thus safety and well being of students is much more important than any other concerns.

Safety hazards.

Any danger or threat to life becomes a hazard. A source that can cause a harm or danger to life becomes a hazard. Although the Possibility of Such threats is in all schools, the residential schools are more vulnerable. Moreover, the parents have handed over their wards to school, hence the entire responsibility of their safety and security is of school. Many unfortunate happenings have been noticed in several schools causing physical harm, mental or emotional harm to the students including loss of life. Therefore, the school authorities have to view this area very seriously failing which any untoward incident can occur. There can be a number of safety hazards depending on the location, climate, discipline, environment, of the school.

Health Hazards.

A residential school as said earlier is a Home Away from Home. Utmost care is taken to look after the students. But sudden illness of hostelers may not be attended as immediately as at home. The junior students are not very serious about such issues and don't bring minor ailments to the notice of concerned HM. Sometimes it becomes serious, causing a threat to life. Similarly fever, cough and cold, stomach pain and many other sickness problems may also pose a threat. The concerned officials have to be very attentive towards this particular issue.

Water bodies.

Some schools are situated near water bodies such as rivers, ponds, lakes etc. Though Residential Schools have a very strong mechanism to control untoward happenings yet The adolescents have a tendency to sneak out and take risk to enjoy bathing and jumping. There have been many incidents of drowning in schools. Day schools also face similar problems but the schools are not responsible for after school incidents.

Bullying.

This is a very common safety hazard in schools. Mostly it is through seniors but sometimes can be through teachers also. As per the education code and school's instructions bullying is strictly prohibited. But it happens indirectly in several forms. It can **be both Physical and Verbal. Both can** cause serious damage. Students can be physically hurt as well as mentally and emotionally disturbed. They don't complain due to the fear and keep it to themselves. If not noticed, attended at the earliest, can become hazardous.

Bunking/Running away.

Bunking can be due to homesickness, bullying, non-adjustment, poor performance or any other factor. The students look for the proper time to run away from the hostel. Maybe for home or elsewhere. In transit they may meet with an accident, may be kidnapped, may be physically or asexually harmed. Often such incidents have occurred in several schools. If not tackled immediately, it can be very dangerous. They have the tendency of fleeing on wee hours. Hence the roll call and feedback systems have to be very strong and effective.

Fire incidents.

Such incidents take place due to negligence and short circuit. Sometimes fire is so devastating that it becomes uncontrollable. In every school there is provision of fire extinguishers even then the incidents happen. Children may get injured, burnt or even lose life. On such times stempede is major cause of fatalities.

Natural disasters.

Earthquakes, floods, pandemics, epidemics, tsunamis, cyclones etc also pose danger to the safety of students. The occurance of such disasters may be rare but the preparedness and precautions are must. Hence the school authorities have to give a serious thought to all such incidents.

Rain borne diseases.

Monsoon Mania is another hazard. Though the rains provide relief from scratching heat yet it introduces unique challenges and several health hazards. From waterborne diseases/illnesses to road safety concerns, this season demands special precautions for our safety and well being. Stagnant water can become breeding grounds for mosquitoes, causing diseases like dengue and malaria. Contaminated water raises the risk of gastro problems. To stay healthy , it's important to maintain good hygiene, clean water and food must be served.

Fights/Quarrels.

There can be individual or group clashes in class or hostel. The youngsters these days are not very tolerant, they lose temper and indulge in fights causing harm to themselves and others. These can become very severe also.

Food poisoning.

This is also one of the common threats in residential schools. The food served to the staff and students is the same. It can be due to the contaminated water or poor quality of fruits, vegetables, cooking carelessness or any other. It can adversely affect the health of many students.

Electric Shocks.

This is most dangerous and can prove to be very fatal. It can be due to lose wiring, contacts, poor maintenance, high voltage or negligence on the part of students and staff. Shocks are so severe that any type of first aid doesn't work. These are life threatening.

Suicides.

Any incident that is most unfortunate and shocking is suicide or attempt to suicide. There are several instances in schools when students lost their lives. There can be many reasons. Poor academic performance, teasing, homesickness, parents indifferent attitude, non adjustment and many others.

Besides, Laboratory accidents- exposure to chemicals, play field accidents- slips, fractures, injuries, adventure sports risks, swimming, horse riding, hiking, trekking, unsafe water, addiction etc are some other safety hazards. Snake, scorpion, stray dog bites can also become hazardous.

Safety and Security Measures.

The hazards need to be dealt effectively and efficiently to provide a safe, healthy and peaceful environment to the students. They are far from their parents who have handed them to school for their education and well-being. Therefore, it becomes the foremost responsibility of the school authority to take proper care of them. Therefore, very comprehensive and exhaustive measures are required to be adopted for the safety and security of students.

Preventive and Proactive Approach.

Staying informed and proactive not only safeguards our well being but also contributes to creating a safer community environment. Prevention is the best remedy. All relevant preventive measures if adopted timely can check all such mishaps in the school. Staff and students must be instructed and trained about all such precautions. All loopholes must be plugged. Extensive training sessions, briefings and frequent interactions with the students can be some proactive measures. Proper records of visitors, movements of students and teachers, and their ID cards are some of the essentials.

Cleanliness drive, proper sanitation, clearing the grass and bushes in and around must be taken up from time to time. Therefore, a more stringent system is needed.

Gated Campus.

Entire campus of the school must be properly fenced from all sides. The boundary wall should have appropriate length and breadth so that it is not possible to sneak out or in. The security arrangements at the gate and in and around the school is of paramount importance. CCTV cameras in sensitive places must be installed. Trespassing and thorough fare should be strictly prohibited.

Out of bond areas

There must be clear cut instructions in the school bylaws about the prohibited areas. Their accessibility must not be easy. Close vigil is required on the students so that they strictly follow the instructions about these areas. All such areas as water bodies, overhead and underground tanks, transformers, gas Chambers, electric panels, solar panels must be declared as out of bound and completely ban the entry of students.

Timely inspection of electric wires, fittings, panels.

To prevent shocks, loose contacts, Short circuits etc , timely inspection and supervision is very essential. Sometimes it is taken casually. This casual approach may cause very severe damage in the form of injury, unconsciousness.

Health and Hygiene.

Nutrition, wellness, prevention, precautions, protection are the necessities of good health. Every child must have a proper cumulative health record. Schools are required to arrange timely health checks. A dispensary, MI room with proper beds depending on the strength of school, proper first aid system are some of the essentials. A regular or visiting qualified and experienced Doctor must be appointed. The parents should be informed immediately about the sickness of students. Minor ailments and injuries must be viewed and dealt seriously.

Students must be taught that **Healthy living is a habit.** It is our responsibility and completely in our hands. *According to Spiritual Guru Sri Sri Ravishankar, ' Your Body is Your Life Partner. Always stays with you. The more you care for your body the more your body will care for you. It is your most valuable asset or otherwise can become the biggest liability for you.'*

First Aid.

It is immediate help soon after any injury, accident, faints, shock or any other casuality. Every school has its own first aid system. After giving first aid the parents are informed immediately and the child is handed over to them. But in a residential school where the students are there 24×7 hrs, first aid is of paramount fimportance. Every school must have a full fledged first aid system including a dispensary, MI room with a suitable number of beds depending on the number of students, medical attendant/ staff nurse, school doctor/visiting doctor. There must be facilities of at least equal to a Public Health Centre. All teachers must be imparted training in health care and first aid and some of them need thorough training. All teachers as well as students need to understand ABC of first Aid ie Airways, Breathing and Circulation.

Hand Wash.

Hand washing is a small action with big impact. According to an estimate eighty percent common infections are transmitted through hands. Hand is perhaps one of the main sources of several diseases. Some of hand transmitted diseases are infections, influenza, gastro problems, cold and cough etc. Germs are transmitted by touch. Students have to be educated about these touches and contacts. It can be one of the important measures. It has been noticed that the students are not very particular about hand washing. Many students don't wash their hands and many of them don't Wash properly. Therefore, demo sessions on hand washing must be arranged. Students need to be taught the importance of hand wash and the style of proper hand wash. Washing hands before and after meals and after using the toilet is a must. **Incorporating proper handwashing into our daily routine is one of the simplest yet most effective ways to maintain health and prevent diseases.**

Monitoring and Feedback.

All steps taken and measures adopted need proper monitoring by the school authorities. Non Compliance of instructions, carelessness on the part of students and concerned staff, discrepancies if any must not be overlooked. Feedback mechanisms should be strengthened in such a manner that any mishap comes in the notice of competent authority.

Counseling Sessions.

Students of tender age and adolescents are often not very serious about all such threats and dangers. Therefore, need to be counselled and guided regularly. Such counselling is very useful for the proper adjustment of students who have come from the home environment to a new one. For emotional support, handling anxiety and stress services of professional counselors have to be managed.

Strong and Robust Visiting System.

Although only the registered visitors are allowed to visit the students yet there are the instances of picking up children by strangers. The security system must be reliable. Strong and Effective.

Escort Duties.

A number of incidents have occurred because of carelessness of escorts in times of movement from one place to another for participation in sports and other activities. There have also been cases of sexual and gender harassment. Female escorts invariably be deputed with girls.

Safety Audit.

It is very necessary to ascertain that the rules and regulations about safety and security are being scrupulously implemented or not. As well as whether the measures adopted are sufficient or not. To maintain checks and balances safety audit is a must exercise to be conducted from time to time. This will enable the school administration to further improve upon this particular issue. Safety audits will strengthen and empower the school community in the creation of a safe, peaceful and healthy environment.

Regulations do not imply merely laying down the rules but their implementation in letter and spirit is must. These rules are formulated keeping in mind all dangers, possible threats and challenges but very easily violated. Therefore, all stakeholders have to cooperate and coordinate with each other so that the children are safe in the premises and feel at home. **Failure if any in this regard is collective inability.**

CHAPTER VI

Mess Management

"A Hungry Person is an Angry Person."

When we say that Residential School is a Home but Away from Home, it must give the feelings of being at home. Besides others, food is the part and partial of generating such feelings. At home, parents take every care to provide quality meals to their children so that they achieve proper physical and mental growth . But when their wards are sent to a Boarding School they expect the same from the school. Therefore, providing a balanced and nutritious diet to the students is the responsibility of the school. Every Residential School has its own mess. Effective mess system is as important as quality education and a safe and secured environment. The children can do well in academics and co-curricular activities only when quality meals are provided. **Healthy mind in healthy body is directly related to healthy food.**

Mess Management is similar to all other areas of management of school functioning such as academic management, classroom management, activities management, finance management and others. Management is to manage men, money and materials. It is to get the work done. Mess management is to run the mess efficiently and effectively. Procurement of materials, qualify check, mess menu preparation of meals, dining system, cleanliness, mess discipline, providing meals timely, mess budget, self-service, dress code, curbing wastage and several other directly or indirectly related areas are the integral components of mess management. Incase the mess affairs are not handled properly, the entire functioning of the school can be adversely affected. Students, particularly seniors, can create any nuisance if they are not satisfied with the meals provided.

The important components of Mess Management are discussed as under....

Mess infrastructure

In every Residential School mess is set up either in a separate building or a specious portion of the hostel. It is generally centrally located so that accessibility is easier. A full fledged mess has sufficient accommodation for kitchen, dining hall, store and cleaning area. Furniture, utensils, cooking appliances, gas chambers, drinking water, wash rooms etc are the essential parts of mess infrastructure. Timely upkeep, maintenance and cleanliness of mess are the important parts of mess management.

Mess Staff

Mess is run with the collective efforts of Mess Employees. The number of cooks, helpers and others is in accordance with the number of students and entitled staff of the school. Mess or Catering Manager supervises and guided the Mess staff in timely preparation of meals, quality and quantity, cleanliness and service. Mess is one of the important pillars of Residential School. Students can be satisfied, happy and can do well in scholastic and co scholastic spheres only when they are provided good meals. This depends on the ability, sincerity and commitment of the mess staff. The school must appreciate the good and hard work done by the mess staff, motivate them and award/reward them suitably.

This is the category of staff that performs the hardest task from early morning till late evening. They are not very well paid. Therefore, this becomes an earnest duty of the school administration to look after their welfare and keep them satisfied and Happy.

Mess Committee

Mess of a Residential School functions under the supervision of a school level committee. It is headed by The Principal.

The vice Principal/ Senior most teacher can be its secretary.

The House Masters, House Prefects, Head boy, head girl , Catering Manager, School Doctor/staff nurse and some selected students are the members

The committee is responsible for the overall functioning of the mess. It supervises all the affairs of mess. It ensures timely procurement, preparation and distribution of meals, cleanliness, mess discipline etc.

Planning, Preparation and Presentation of meals

Planning for effective functioning of a mess is one of the crucial components of mess management. Planning includes:

Procurement process

Groceries, vegetables, milk, fruits and all other items are procured in advance through the process of tendering/ quotations. Quality and quantity are the main concerns of this process. There is a school level committee for this purpose.

Preparation of Menu

Menu is the list of food items served in the mess on a day to day basis. It is planned and prepared in such a way that all items of the meals useful for proper nutrition are covered. All meals including the items provided are prescribed in the menu. All three meals, snacks, fruits, special meals on special occasions are clearly listed in the menu. It is the responsibility of the mess committee to ensure that the prescribed menu is scrupulously followed. There can be some seasonal changes as per the availability of fruits and vegetables.

Preparation of Meals

Food being served in the mess should not only be good for the tongue but it should also be good for the eyes. It should be tasty as well as smell and look good. Cleanliness is the serious concern while preparing meals. There must be regular checking of cleanliness in and around the mess and mess staff. The utensils used for cooking as well as the cutlery must also be neat and clean.

It is crucial to consume freshly cooked food, avoiding raw or left over items that may harbor bacteria. Fruit and vegetables must be washed with clean and fresh water.

Quality Checks

Catering to a larger group of students and staff is a challenging and daunting task. Every care has to be taken to check both the quality and quantity of food being served. In case the quantity is not sufficient, any nuisance can take place. Whereas improper quality can cause a big harm. Therefore, daily supervision of both quality and quantity of meals is very essential. Surprise check by the Principal, close vigil by the Catering Supervisor, daily inspection by the House masters, staff nurse and duty teachers will certainly suffice the purpose. **Too spicy can be too tasty but not nutritious.** Oily and spicy food is always avoided in a boarding school.

Dining System

One of the objectives of The Residential School is to promote the feelings of togetherness and belongingness.

The students live, learn and dine together. In a Residential School Dining Hall is attached with mess. It has to be as specious as can accommodate all students at a time. There can be a separate dining for girls. It should be neat, clean, well-ventilated with all physical facilities. The students and teachers take meals together. It is supervised by the Duty Master, Catering Manager and House masters. There is either a self-service system or Table service. Students are also given service duties to enable them to understand dignity of labour.

Dining system is not only meant for having meals but also to learn table manners, good eating habits and serving each other. Dining system helps in cultivating the values of discipline, responsibility, love and peace.

Presentation of meals

Meals prepared should be served in a decent way. Need to be placed properly on the Tables in the dining hall. Personal hygiene is also important while serving the meals.

Cleanliness

There is a famous saying that Cleanliness is Next to Godliness. Utmost efforts are needed to keep Mess surroundings neat and clean. The upkeep of Kitchen, dining hall, and utensils is a must. Proper protection from insects is required. Wire mesh on doors and windows is one of the safety measures. It must be ensured that the students wash their hands before and after every meal. The bushes and grass should be cleaned from time to time.

Mess Discipline

One of the objectives of the dining system is to inculcate the sense of discipline among the students. The duty teachers have to ascertain that the time schedule of the mess must strictly be followed. The staff and students must report on time for meals. Keeping silence in the dining hall is essential. Table manners, discipline, decorum, orderly behaviour becomes exemplary.

Mess Budget

Budget is an integral component of mess management. Every school fixes the norms for meals provided. Every care is taken to serve a balanced and nutritious diet to the hostelers within the budget provisions. The school administration monitors and ensures that the funds allocated are used judiciously and effectively.

Curbing wastage

It has been observed that children and youngsters often waste food. They leave it on the table or throw it in the waste bin. They have to be taught and trained about the importance of food and the effects of misuse. Wastage of food may cause shortage as well as filth in and around the mess. There should be a perfect garbage handling system. Proper rapport has to be established with the concerned authority in the nearby area for timely spraying, fogging and garbage removal.

CHAPTER VII

Where Discipline is a Tradition

"Discipline is the Bridge Between Goals and Accomplishments."

Discipline is one of the Fundamental Values. It lays the foundation of success. Unfortunately, in this era of modernization and emerging technologies Generation Gap has become the buzzword. The youngsters by and large don't understand the importance of discipline in life and when the elders make efforts to imbibe this the Phrase Generation Gap comes on their way. However, the Residential System is perhaps the best platform to inculcate discipline. In fact, discipline is one of the traditions of a Residential School.

Discipline word has originated from Disciple which means student. It was meant for education. The students in Gurukul were expected to be disciplined i.e. regulate their behaviour, attitude and action. It is also known as Self Discipline. Of course, even today the foundation of discipline is laid in family and school. But the discipline then and now is somehow different. It was a strict process but gradually has become a lenient one.

Discipline is a process of correction or molding for better behavior and action. It is an action taken to encourage compliance. It grows from within and not without. The best form of discipline is self-discipline. It is a mode of life in accordance with certain values and regulations. It is a state of conduct and behavior of an individual. Discipline is one of the necessities of life to succeed. In a Residential school Discipline is a way of living. The system provides ample opportunities to be disciplined and this sense remains throughout life. It is one of the healthy traditions of the school.

Discipline becomes a habit in a Residential School. Any act of indiscipline is neither acceptable nor tolerable. There are the subsystems of the school through which a close vigil is observed on the inmates. Residential School has a regulatory environment. Rules and regulations are strictly complied with. It is not that the responsibility of discipline is of school administration but the senior students are also involved. School is a home also and therefore; principals and teachers have dual responsibility of both parents and teachers. Schedule is so tight that there is hardly any scope for indulging in one or the other act of indiscipline.

What makes the students of Residential School Disciplined beings?

Discipline is the tradition in Residential School. School earns its name and fame not only owing to its strong academic environment but also of its known discipline in every sphere.

Various subsystems of the school are the greatest tools to cultivate discipline and mannerism amongst the students.

Morning Activities.

Early to bed and early to rise, makes a man healthy, wealthy and wise. Residential School is the best example of this saying. Morning PT, exercises, yoga and meditation sessions are the regular features. These are not only useful for self but also for self and general discipline.

Morning Assembly.

Morning assembly sets the trend for the entire day. Turning together, standing and praying together is the first act of discipline. The Assembly of most of the Residential Schools is very impressive, informative and effective.

Effective House System.

In House the students learn to live together, help each other, self-dependence and belongingness. These all are the attributes of good discipline.

Innovative and Interactive Teaching Learning Practices.

Classroom discipline is very essential. One cannot teach an undisciplined class. The students are taught the importance of discipline in their respective classes.

Friendly Hostel Environment.

In hostel students learn to live together. Sense of discipline automatically prevails.

Effective Dining System.

Dining together and following table manners cultivates discipline.

Self-help/service.

In a Residential School students have to help themselves. They are self-dependent. This trait also makes the students self-disciplined.

Personality Development Program.

Several programs are initiated in a Residential School for personality development. Discipline is an important attribute of personality.

Games and Sports.

Team spirit, sportsmanship, enthusiasm and zeal during games and sports imbibe the sense of discipline in students.

Counseling and Guidance.

Various counseling and guidance sessions organised from time to time also motivate the students to be disciplined.

Parental care, love and affection.

As the parents often instruct, guide and encourage their siblings to adhere to discipline at home, the principals and teachers do the same in school.

Cordial, congenial homely atmosphere.

The conducive and homely environment of a Residential School inspires the students to be disciplined in every sphere.

Types of Discipline.

There can be several types of discipline. The types vary from organization to organization. Can be different in education, administration, police, army and elsewhere. The most common types are...

Preventive Discipline.

This prevents anything wrong from happening in school. The school community is encouraged to follow the prescribed code of discipline so that the standards, rules and regulations are followed.

Corrective Discipline.

It is to mend the ways of students. In other words, action taken in case of non-compliance. Maybe a penalty, fine, suspension etc.

Supportive Discipline.

In case of any misconduct, misbehavior, the students are given a chance to explain. If need be, provided assistance to put forward their views.

Restorative Discipline.

It is to establish a relationship with the students. It can be of a parent, teacher or guide. They are strengthened so they don't feel isolated.

Different Approaches to Discipline.

Progressive Approach.

This to give a chance to students to correct themselves and improve their conduct. If given in clear but Swift words, it works to a larger extent.

Positive Approach.

It is to make them aware of the future consequences of any act of misconduct or undesirable behaviour.

Constructive Approach.

It is root cause analysis. Main root or cause of the problem is identified before taking any decision or action.

The Residential Schools have stringent rules of maintaining discipline. Without proper discipline no school can function smoothly. But it becomes more important in Residential School where the responsibility doesn't end soon after the school is over. In fact, after school there is more scope for any untoward happening. As long as the students are in their respective classes, by and large no major problem occurs. But the task of teachers is difficult after school hours.

Techniques to Maintain Discipline.

There are several techniques of discipline but differ from school to school depending on their overall functioning. But the most common of them are the following...

Motivational Technique

It is most common and largely experimented and exercised. It works to a larger extent. The students are motivated to behave in a desirable manner. Moral lessons are given to them citing the examples of great people who lead disciplined lives and reach the highest level of success. Moral talks can be delivered in Assembly, classes, hostel, mess, social gathering and elsewhere. Eminent personalities can also be invited to boost the morale of students on special occasions.

Giving them patient hearing, recognizing and affiliating them, helping them in their adjustment and adaptation, parental love and affection are some other motivational techniques.

Reward Techniques

The desirable and acceptable deeds of students must be acknowledged and appreciated even of so-called undisciplined students. Praise, citations, recommendations, prizes, some freedom, responsibility are some of the reward techniques. These techniques go a long way in maintaining discipline. Unfortunately, many schools don't experiment with it and the students of indifferent behavior and conduct remain neglected.

Punishment Techniques

It is the oldest and widely used technique till recently. It **is based on the old adage,' spare The Rod and Spoil the Child.'** It firmly believes that offenders deserve to be punished. It has been happening since long and continued till corporal punishment was banned by an act. This is based on different theories....

Retributive Theory.

Let the culprit suffer and face the punishment for wrong doings. It believes in **'An eye to an eye' and a 'tooth to a tooth'.**

Vindictive Theory.

Law is supreme and it will take its own course. Whatever may be the cause, the offender must be punished in accordance with the law meant to curb it.

Preventive Theory.

It is based on the famous saying, **'Prevention is better than cure,'.** Efforts must be made to prevent any indiscipline from taking place. Proactive approach is required.

Some forms of punishment...

Verbal punishment.

Words are the strongest weapons. If uttered timely, genuinely and positively, the words can do wonders. It is said that the fear is in the voice and eyes of the teachers. Most teachers mend the ways of learners via this and succeed to a greater extent.

Non-verbal Punishment.

Body language, gesture, posture and eye contact are also of great significance. Teachers demonstrate such body language that the students easily understand the temperament of the teacher. They stop themselves from doing anything wrong.

The above forms may work in case of minor problems and with the junior students. May or may not help in case of seniors. More stringent strategies are required.

Detention and suspension

In case of some serious cases, the students can be detained or suspended for certain period. They must be given time to realize and improve.

Fines/Replacement.

For any damage to the school asset the students can be fined or asked to replace/repair the damaged thing.

Withdrawal of scholarship, privileges

In case the students are availing some scholarship or privilege, it can be withdrawn for any indulgence in indiscipline.

Moral punishment

Seeking an apology in public is a great insult. Generally, it demotivates but sometimes becomes necessary.

Corporal Punishment in any form is strictly prohibited. In case exercised in some extreme situation, the handlers must be prepared to face the music.

51

CHAPTER VIII

Daily Routine of a Residential School

"The secret of your future is hidden in your daily routine

Mike Murdock"

The basic philosophy of a Residential School is to keep students gainfully busy. The functioning of the school will be smooth and effective only when the students are engaged. Every School has its own time and activities schedule. But it is somehow different as well as hectic in case of Residential School. Daily routine is a time schedule of day-to-day functioning of the school. It is prepared keeping in view the following.

Engagement of students and staff in different tasks.

Following the time allotted to each activity strictly.

Achieving good results.

Accomplishment of the vision and mission of the school.

Establishing a good rapport with each other.

The routine of all Residential Schools is almost similar. There can be slight changes. The routine of summer and winter can also have some changes.

A suggestive Daily Routine is appended below

Rouser............................5.15 AM

PT Exercises....................5.45 A M

Change/Bath....................6.45 A M

Breakfast........................7.30AM

Assembly........................8 A M

First Four Periods (40 mins each) 8.40 to 11.20 AM
Short Break (fruits can be served) 11.20 -11.35 AM
V and VI periods (40 mins each)11. 35 to 12 .45PM
Last two periods of 35 minutes each..12.45 PM to 1. 55 PM

Lunch.............................2 to 2.40 PM
Rest...........................2.40PM to 4.0 PM
Remedial/Enrichment Teaching 4 to 5 PM
(Remedial for underachievers and Enrichment for High Achievers).
Games/Sports........................5 to 6PM
Bath/Change.........................6 to 6.30PM
Supervised Studies..........6.30 to 8.15 PM
Evening Assembly and Roll Call...8.20 PM
Dinner........................... 8.30to 9 PM
Self Studies in Hostel/Houses..9 To 10 PM
Lights Off.............................10. 15 PM
Let us discuss every aspect of the routine

Rouser..

'Morning Hour has gold in its mouth'.

Benjamin Franklin

The students have to get up soon after ringing the Rouser bell as per the routine. They have to follow the Army like time and discipline. Residential Schools are the firm believers of the old saying,' **Early to bed and early to rise, makes you healthy wealthy and wise.'**

PT/Exercises.

The Physical Training Instructors start blowing the whistle to alert the students. They fall in lines in the main ground of the School. Besides P.T is, MOD(Master on Duty) one or two House Masters alternatively remain present. House wise Roll call is taken. Presence of every student is ensured. Information of sick house members is reported by the House Prefects. **Thus the hustle and bustle begins in the school in the early morning hours.**

The students are made to run, exercise, and mass PT. This is compulsory for all students. It takes about half an hour. In the remaining time the students practice their games/sports.

Breakfast.

This is the second activity after morning exercises. After finishing their bath students turn up for breakfast on the scheduled time in school uniform. They have to finish their breakfast within the stipulated time. HMs, MOD and catering manager perform the supervising duties. The entitled category of teachers also dine with the students.

Morning Assembly.

Soon after breakfast students assemble in the ground or assembly hall. They fall in lines either house or class wise. At random attendance is taken by the class teachers/house. Masters. The Assembly of Residential **Schools is always very impressive, innovative and informative. Almost all suggestive activities are conducted in the assembly.**

Teaching learning process in first half

As mentioned in the time schedule, the first four periods of 40 minutes each are conducted. Academic time table is prepared in such a manner that the subjects needing deep thinking, understanding and attention are taught in the morning as Math, Science, English, Accountancy etc. The Residential Schools focus on innovative, interactive and transformative teaching learning. They don't overburden the students with plenty of homework.

Short Break.

After completion of fourth period, students are given a short break of about fifteen to twenty minutes. They collect their books and copies from their dormitories for the subjects taught after a short break. The House masters, PT teacher and MOD keep close vigil on the movements of students and make every effort to curb any incident of indiscipline.

Four periods in the second half.

Rest of the subjects are taught in this half. Periods for subjects having lower difficulty level are allotted in this half. Owing to a hectic schedule since morning, students may get tired also. Therefore, the teachers are competent enough to entertain them by subject related humour, activities, stories etc.

Lunch Break.

After concluding the academic time table students keep their bags in their houses and without wasting any time turn up in the dining hall for lunch. Lunch is served as per the menu for the day. Again, the MOD, HMS and mess manager supervise them.

Rest Hour.

Students go back to their hostels after lunch. It is some rest time for them after busy academic hours. This is their Own Time also. The youngsters generally don't take rest they rather enjoy, gossip, talk about classroom happenings and thus get rid of day's mental fatigue.

Remedial and Enrichment Teaching.

After refreshing themselves for about an hour and half again report back to their respective classrooms for Remedial and Enrichment Programs. There is never a homogeneous group in the class. Some are underachievers whereas some are high achievers. Remedial teaching is for under achievers who need some special attention and suggestive capsules in the subjects in which their performance is not up to the level. The Enrichment program is for the gifted ones who need higher order thinking capsules.

Evening Games and Sports.

This is a period of about an hour or an hour and half. All students are engaged in one or the other games/sports activities. Teachers also participate as per their interest. Every child has to be on the ground. Fortunately there are facilities for most of the games. Students enjoy this period and take part with zeal and enthusiasm. Sometimes matches between students and teachers are also organized in this period.

Supervised Studies.

After the games period the students go to their respective houses, quickly change and come back to the Academic Block for supervised studies. Supervised in the sense that the studies are conducted under the supervision of teachers. This period is about one and half or two hrs. Students complete their homework, revise, prepare for next day and work on the projects given to them. Some subject teachers along with MOD perform supervised studies duty. If need be they help the students in their respective subjects. The purpose is not to teach but supervise and help.

Evening Assembly.

After the supervised studies again, the students gather in the ground. Roll call is taken in the presence of House Masters and Prayer is conducted.

Dinner.

Students keep their books in their dorms and quickly go to the dining hall. Their seating arrangement is house wise. There can be a separate dining hall for girls. In the dining hall there is either table service or self-service.

Principal frequently takes rounds during almost all the activities to monitor and gather feedback.

Self-Studies.

After dinner the students have about one hour at their disposal. They remain in the hostel. Do their rest of the work, revise, study themselves or have their own time.

Lights Off.

Roundabout at ten fifteen or ten thirty there is an alarm for lights off. All students have to switch off their lights and go to sleep. The principal and H.Ms may also go for surprise checks.

The daily routine of the Residential Schools is therefore, very hectic. The students are kept gainfully busy so that they learn at a faster pace, develop their personality and become self-dependent.

CHAPTER IX

Co-Curricular Activities

"All Work and No Play Makes Jack a Dull Boy."

Healthy Mind is in Healthy Body. The saying is very relevant to the Residential Schools where there is equal focus on mental and Physical Development. Various pedagogical programs are for mental development and a variety of co-curricular activities enhance physical fitness , endurance, stamina and strength . The Residential School System provides ample opportunities for both. The daily routine of a Residential School is very hectic because of these activities. These activities are very helpful in wholesome personality development. **A plethora of activities keep them happy, healthy, hearty and energetic.**

The success of a Residential School besides other attributes depends on **'Keeping the Students Gainfully Busy'. In case they are not kept busy they keep the** teachers busy. **'An idle mind is devil's workshop'. It is very true everywhere but much more** relevant to the Residential School System. Therefore, for smooth functioning and yielding better results the students must invariably be kept busy in one or the other activities. **Organization of Cocurricular Activities is the best remedy for every malady.** For participating in these activities, a considerable physical strength and mental fortitude is required.

Previously the school activities were divided in the following categories.

Curricular Activities.

The activities directly related with academics are curricular activities. Teaching, learning, testing, training, evaluation etc. are the curricular activities.

Co Curricular Activities.

The activities indirectly concerned with curriculum such as debate, declamation, dramatics, essay writing, extempore speech, quiz, exhibitions etc. fall in this category.

Extra Co Curricular Activities.

These are the activities having no direct or indirect relation with the above activities. These are games, sports, NCC, NSS, Scout and Guides, Plantation, cleanliness drive etc. are the extracurricular activities.

Some of the suggestive activities are mentioned below:

Physical Development Activities

Games and sports.

'Talents win games but teamwork wins championships'.

Various games and sports activities can be organised in a befitting manner. Fortunately, the Residential Schools have good scope for these activities because of availability of students and teachers twenty four hours and facilities. It is compulsory for every student to participate in on or the other activities. They are not allowed to sit idle in hostels or elsewhere. The schools provide facilities for almost all minor as well as major games and sports.

Major games include football, volleyball, basketball, handball, hockey, cricket, kho-kho, kabaddi, lawn tennis, squash etc. The schools organise these as per the infrastructure and facilities available. Not necessary that every school has facilities for so many games.

Minor games include, table tennis, chess carrom board, ludo etc. There can be indoor facilities for some of the games. Some elite schools provide all facilities including swimming, wrestling, horse riding, gymnastics, boxing and martial art practices such as judo, karate etc.

Sports Activities.

Track and Field Activities.

These activities include sprints, long races, hurdles, staple chase, relays etc.

Jumps.

Long jump, high jump, pole vault, triple jump are some of the activities falling in this category.

Throws.

Shot put, hammer throw, javelin throw, discus throw, ball throw are some throw activities.

Adventure Activities.

Residential schools also aim at making the students rough, tough, bold, courageous and daring. To accomplish this objective a variety of adventure activities are also conducted from time to time. Such as climbing, mountaineering, hiking, cycling, trekking, skiing etc.

Literary Activities.

The purpose of These activities is to strengthen the mental faculties of children and also to boost their confidence, communication skills and other personality attributes. Some of the activities are.

Debate, declamation, extempore speeches, quiz, dramatics, essay writing, poem recitation etc.

Aesthetic Development Activities.

Art, Craft, painting, poster making, decoration etc.

Cultural Activities

These activities promote culture, traditions, heritage and keep students intact with rich heritage. **Music vocal as well as instrumental, dance- solo and group, songs solo and. group, Fancy dress, variety program etc. are some of the suggestive activities in this group.**

Moral Development Activities.

One of the objectives of education is the moral development of students. The schools conduct a number of such activities to achieve this purpose **such as Assembly activities- prayer, pledge, thoughts, mass prayers, story-telling, inviting eminent personalities for talk etc.**

Civic Development Activities.

These are some group activities useful for developing civic sense and understanding the functioning of various institutions delivering community services.

Youth/Mock Parliament, cooperative store, school socials, visit of banks, post office, hospital, police stations, celebration of festivals, school fairs and fate, celebration of national days, camping etc.

Leisure Time Activities.

In a Residential School the schedule is so tight that the students hardly have any spare or leisure time at their disposal. Even then whatever time they get from their busy schedule they can cultivate their hobbies of **stamp, coin, fossil collection, scrapbook, poster, painting making etc.**

Productive Activities.

These are the learn and earn activities. In some of the schools these activities are conducted for skill development The products produced are displayed in school exhibitions, fairs, annual days and fêtes. **These include book binding, chalk and soap making, wood craft, knitting, tailoring, weaving etc. Previously these were known as Socially useful productive work (SUPW)**

Extra co-curricular Activities.

These activities are other than the above activities. Their significance in personality development is equally important. Such activities play a dominating role in developing leadership qualities, dignity of labor, sense of social service, patriotism etc. **Some of these activities are:**

National Cadet Corps (NCC)

In independent India, a need to impart military type training to the youngsters of schools and colleges was felt. To fulfil this objective NCC was founded in 1948. It has all three wings of defence forces i.e. Army, Navy and Air Force. The schools and colleges are free to choose these wings. NCC activities include parades, camps, firing as well as some social and community services. Its motto is '**Unity and Discipline**'. NCC builds self-confidence, commitment and creates feelings of patriotism.

National Service Scheme (NSS)

It came into being in 1969 under the ministry of Youth Affairs and Sports. NSS volunteers play a vital role in National Service towards Blood Donations, Sharmdans, afforestation, natural disasters and cleanliness drives. The objectives are character building, personality development, voluntary community services etc.

Scout and Guides

It was started in 1914 to develop life skills and value orientation. Now it is known as Bharat Scouts and Guides. Scouts are the boys and girls are the Guides.

Scientific Attitude Development Activities.

Science quizzes, exhibitions, fairs, visits to science cities and scientific institutions are some of the activities to develop scientific temperament and attitude.

Educational excursions.

This is an integral component of Residential School. Excursions are organised to give students some respite from a busy academic schedule. They enjoy and learn during these excursions.

Sharmdaans

Students can also be engaged in voluntary service in school and the community. They understand the dignity of labour and contribute something to the on-going works

Community Cooking.

In times of school picnics students can be given some work such as chopping, cutting, cleaning etc. On Sundays and holidays senior students can help the mess staff in cooking.

Besides, Students can also be taken to zoos, museums, national parks, bird sanctuaries etc.

Now the above classification of CCA has been summed up as

Scholastic Activities i.e. the curricular activities or the pedagogical activities.

And

Co Scholastic Activities i.e. all other co-curricular and extracurricular activities.

Inter House and Inter School Competitions.

Inter house competitions are organized throughout the year. House points are recorded and added at the time of concluding the competitions. The house getting maximum points is declared as the **Champion or Cock House.**

Similarly Inter School Competitions are organised once a year. The school systems having a chain of schools as Navodaya Vidyalayas, Kendriya Vidyalayas, Sainik Schools, DAV Schools organise these competitions on Cluster, Regional and National Basis. Selected Schools also participate in **SGFI i.e. Schools Games Federation of India.**

Thus CCA is one of the strongest pillars of Residential Schools. These activities foster team spirit, sportsmanship, zeal for competition, leadership, discipline, unity and strength. **True competition Kindle self-actualization and prepares to enjoy the win and accept the defeat.**

CHAPTER X

Excellence is the Buzzword

"Excellence is never an accident. It is always the result of high intentions, sincere efforts and intelligent execution. It represents the wise choice of many alternatives. Choice, not Chance determines your destiny.

Aristotle"

The foremost objective of a Residential School is to strive for excellence in every sphere. In fact in this era of cut throat competition, excellence has become the need of the hour. It is not academic excellence only but the purpose is to prepare the students to excel in almost all fields so that the school is able to give back the parents a fine, well groomed, cultured, mannered and disciplined person who is prepared to face the challenges of life and avail any opportunity knocking at his/her door steps. High performing Institutions are known for their legacy of Excellence. **This excellence achieved in school converts a person into a Personality.**

It is not the facilities, infrastructure and quality education but also the willpower to do something unique. Most of the great people have not succeeded because of the facility but because of the difficulty.

'Born in a landless family, mother of three, Olympian, Asian Champion and Rajya Sabha M P Marry Com accomplished what she desired.'

What is Excellence?

Quality of being extremely good is excellent. Doing something extraordinary and achieving the highest results. Excellence is to leave far behind the competitors. Excellence is the competition with self. Doing much better than before. Excellence is to have your own pace of performance. Excellence is the result of smart work, dedication, perseverance and commitment. Having capabilities of giving sterling performance is excellence. Quality leads to excellence and therefore, because of quality education the students of Residential School excel in academics, CCA and elsewhere. It is a beacon of excellence. Almost all subsystems of a Residential School make earnest efforts to achieve excellence in their respective areas. **The school thus becomes the school of Eminence, Prominence and Excellence.**

All students have competency to excel but the efforts, hard work, and attention differ from each other. Road to success is often dotted with obstacles but needs a lot of grit to reach the destination. **Excellence is not only a tradition but becomes a habit. These** days work pressure has increased manifold. Horizons of education are expanding into new exciting realms. The Residential Schools provide supporting and facilitating learning environments. to the inmates. There is good scope and several opportunities to excel. Emphasis is on development of soft skills. Provides a supportive and facilitating atmosphere of learning. The picturesque and enchanting location of the schools help in learning some pertinent lessons of life. Schools deliver the training of head, heart and soul. Students achieve the milestone through meticulously planned teaching learning strategies and unique support systems.

'Choice not chance Determines Your Destiny'.
Aristotle

Excellence is never an accident. It doesn't happen by chance. It is always the result of high intention, sincere efforts and intelligent execution of ideas. It comes out of the wise choice of many alternatives. Unmatched proficiency and hassle-free culture carry the legacy of excellence forward.

Students are trained to 'do their best and leave the rest to God or destiny'.

Bhagwad Gita.

Every student is prepared to achieve the benchmark and strengthen the prestige and pride of the school.

Academic Excellence.

Most of the schools focus on academic excellence. Some succeed and some do not. Achieving good results, producing meritorious students and bringing name and fame are the important objectives of all schools. But for a Residential School it is somehow different. Its purpose is not excellence in academics but all affairs. **Academic Excellence is the result of well-planned teaching learning strategies, carefully conceived curriculum, confident, committed and competent teachers, innovative, interactive and learner centered teaching. Residential Schools achieve this through quality education.**

Components of Excellence.

There are many components which determine excellence or Students achieve excellence because of the following

Self Confidence.

To live without hope is to cease to live.

The first and foremost requirement to excel is self-confidence. It is to have trust in oneself. Believing the competencies and talents of self. Having a high self-esteem and understanding self. The tradition and overall-environment of Residential Schools foster self-confidence. The students participate in a number of activities with interest. They are trained to celebrate the victory and gladly accept the defeat. The culture of the residential system is such that it breeds confidence and hope. The students are hopeful of their success. Hope enhances confidence and confidence breeds excellence. **Hope is an emotion that keeps us in motion. Hope is a good thing, may be the best thing and good things never die.**

Knowledge, Skills and Attitude.

To excel in any field one must have thorough knowledge of the concerned area, Skills to Deal with that and a will or attitude to achieve. Students can excel in academics only when they have grasped their subjects thoroughly, have necessary skills to prepare and score good marks and have the attitude to deliver. It applies to other fields also.

Quality of Teachers.

Quality Education is a far cry in absence of quality teachers. The residential schools select the teachers through a rigorous recruitment process. They don't compromise on their teaching aptitude, knowledge and desirable experience. Quality breeds excellence and every residential school strives for it. It is not only the quality of teaching faculty but also all support staff. For academic excellence effective and efficient teachers are required. At the same time good physical training instructors and coaches are required to excel in games and sports. **Quality teachers produce Quality Students.**

Quality leadership.

One can excel only when the direction and guidance is perfect. A good leader can direct, guide and motivate. Both Principal and teachers are able to provide good leadership which helps students to excel in various fields. Leadership is not to create followers but to create more leaders. It filters downwards from Principal to teachers and students. Residential Schools prepare future leaders who excel in their walks of life.

Discipline lays the foundation

Excelling in any field is impossible without a Disciplined System and Self Discipline. It has already been stated that Discipline is a Tradition in Residential Schools. There is an environment of discipline in and around the school which results in students' discipline. No stone is unturned to cultivate the sense of self discipline amongst the students and staff.

Strong Support System.

It is not only the quality of manpower but also the facilities i.e. infrastructure, labs, library, play fields and physical facilities...sanitation, potable water, electricity, quality meals, safety and security, health and hygiene etc. It doesn't mean that in absence of all these facilities one can not excel. As the saying goes, **'Great people are not the product of facility but of adversity'**. There are also gifted ones. They excel whatever the circumstance may be.

Vision and Mission.

Both the vision and mission of Residential Schools aim at **'Doing better than before'**. They themselves are their competitors. Excellence is their motto in both Vision and Mission. They always strive to accomplish it and prepare their students accordingly.

Smart work replaces the Hard Work.

In Residential Schools both teacher and taught don't work hard only but work smartly. Their approach to achievement is always smart and different from others. Both are goal oriented. **Where there is a will there's a way'. A strong will not only to succeed but to excel is**

created. They believe in Questioning. The students throw challenges to teachers and the students are encouraged to raise questions to remove their doubts. This is not only in academics but elsewhere also. Both have a quest for excellence.

"I love the word 'Question' because it has 'Quest' in it'. "
Eleve Wiesel (Nobel Laureate)
Efforts and initiations.

Both initiation and consistency are two important factors to succeed. Our mythology as well as history has several instances of initiatives, hard work and efforts that never go in vain. The story of Hanuman is very relevant in this context...

In Ramayana Jatayu the Vulture told Rama about Sita. When Hanuman gave up the hope to discover Sita, he was disappointed and thought that Rama, Laxman and Sugriv would die of sorrow. He wanted to commit suicide. Sitting near the sea he saw a small bird taking flight towards the ocean again and again. He asked the bird the reason behind it. The bird replied 'My nest fell in the ocean, I want to dry it up. Hanuman got the inspiration and continued his efforts. He found Sita.

Communication Skills.

Residential Culture is hassle free. Students have full freedom to interact with their Principal and teachers. They are free and frank. This type of liberty develops communication skills. They are encouraged to come forward with their queries in the classroom, play field and elsewhere. They don't hesitate to share, are open minded and confident about the solution. Good communication is perhaps the greatest attribute of personality development as well as to excel. It fosters intelligible dialogue between two or more persons.

Communication is not simply interaction or exchange of ideas and thoughts but an expression of deeper understanding of each other. The most important tool of communication is personal interactions. This is the most positive communication and yields desired results. Many problems arise due to failure of communication at any stage or miscommunication or communication gap. Effective communication doesn't only bring positive changes but also builds good relationships and motivates the students and teachers to excel.

Effective communication has to be brief, meaningful, clear, simple, impressive, understandable, vivid and adequate.

Motivation.

To excel one must feel motivated. Fortunately, there are a number of motivators in Residential Schools. There is a highly motivated team of principals and teachers. The culture of Residential Schools is such that the students are always bubbling with enthusiasm, they are happy and feel motivated. Students are self-motivated as well as get motivation from their teachers and principal from time to time. Motivation always creates an urge to excel.

Motivation can be of two types

Intrinsic Motivation.

It comes from within. An urge to succeed. It is also known as self-motivation.

Extrinsic Motivation.

It comes from outside i.e. the teachers, principals, parents and peers in terms of praise, appreciation, citation, recommendations.

Thus, the students of a Residential School become competent enough to manage themselves, their studies and activities. **They are able to balance all of these and** therefore, the scope to excel is much more. Higher level of intelligence, competence, confidence, adequate preparation, indomitable determination, will power, a burning desire to succeed are some of the attributes of the students of Residential School which lead them to excellence.

CHAPTER XI

Personality Development

"Don't live like a person, live like a Personality. Person will die one day, personality will live forever"

The ultimate aim of Education is Personality Development of Child. It is an integral part of all education policies, part and partial of school vision and mission and endeavor of every Principal and teacher. Although all schools aim at Personality Development yet the Residential Schools provide a much better environment for holistic personality development. Almost all subsystems of a Residential School significantly contribute towards Personality Development. The House System, variety of activities, discipline, self-confidence and an urge to excel are some of the important contributors.

What is Personality?

For a lay person personality may be.

Social Attractiveness.

One who looks attractive, impressive, smart, handsome and beautiful. Like a film or sports personality.

Physical appearance?

One who is tall, stout and stubborn.

The way one talks, acts or behaves and thinks.

Character, values and habits of a Person.

Personality is in fact combination of all above. The combine virtues that make a person different from others.

If we see it in the context of Residential Schools, the teachers and students are tuned to possess all these attributes. The person with a good personality is one who impresses others with his/her social skills and effectiveness. **Gordon Allport has very aptly defined personality as**

'Personality is the dynamic organization within the individual of those Psycho Physical systems that determine the unique adjustment to his/her environment'.

We can analyze the definition of Gordon Allport as under...

Organization.

It refers to self i.e. sum of all personality traits. These traits combine together to make a full personality.

Psycho Physical.

Mental and Physical systems.

This is the mental and physical being. These two are the important dimensions of personality. Good personality consists of intelligence, alertness and healthy habits.

Determinants.

The factors that determine one's personality. These are several in number and leave an indelible impact on one's personality.

Unique.

Differs from others. All people are not alike. Even the twins differ from each other

Adjustment.

As per the circumstances and situation people make efforts to adjust and adapt. Non adjustment with the prevailing circumstances hampers one's personality development.

Characteristics.

All people have different characteristics. These features of the personality of a person may also differ from each other.

Personality development is self-development. On the basis of the above discussion of personality, there are five dimensions of personality.

Physical Self.

It is a very important dimension of personality. A developed personality is certainly a physically fit, stout and healthy person. All other dimensions can be developed only when one maintains good health. The first concern of the parents is the health of their children. They do everything to keep them healthy even if they cannot afford it. When we have said that Residential School is a Home Away From Home, the health of students becomes the primary concern of the school. Besides nutritious food the schools have several programs to keep the hostelers physically fit.

Energy Self.

Looking healthy is not sufficient to be physically fit. Along with healthy looks one must have sufficient energy to go along. Good food is not the only source of Energy. It comes out of the will to perform, being positive and motivational practices. Lot of energy is required to study, play, participate in CCA and other activities. We need different energies for different activities. In a Residential School, efforts are made not only to keep the students physically fit but also to keep them energetic.

Mental Self.

Healthy mind in a healthy body applies everywhere. We Can strengthen our mental self only by being physically fit. Keeping fit is the basic philosophy of Residential

Schools. They make every effort to keep them physically fit and mentally strong and alert. Reading, writing, listening, reasoning, general awareness, communication, self-confidence, self-reliance are all mental dimensions of personality. Residential Schools strive to make the inmates mentally strong through various school activities.

Intellectual Self.

Though intelligence is a god gift yet physical and mental fitness is also important to be intelligent. One can be very intelligent but due to poor health and lack of proper energy one cannot express it.

Blissful Self.

It is devotion towards chosen ideals. '**Work is worship**', is the crux of this self. Whatever you do with devotion, commitment and determination. It is also to perform assigned tasks happily and peacefully. We may find happiness in practicing hobbies, playing, music etc.

There can be two types of personality.

Inner Personality.

This is our internal self. It cannot be seen and observed at once. Our thinking, value base, beliefs and character are some of the traits of our inner personality.

Outer Personality.

This is noticeable and can be observed. The way we look, talk and behave are some of the traits.

Introvert Personality.

Being with oneself is introversion. Such persons are less talkative, hesitant, shy, think more talk less, they are imaginative and creative. They have few friends and don't like to mix up with others. They are good listeners, concentrate and pay attention.

Extrovert Personality.

Mixing up with large groups and talking and sharing with them is extroversion. Such people are talkative and try to impress others by making them listen.

Personality Traits.

Every person inherits personality traits from heredity and environment.

Hereditary Traits.

These are the traits which one inherits from parents and blood relations from mother or father sides. These can be alike or similar. Such as physique- height, weight, stature- tall or short, colour, eyes, nose, walks, talks, temperament and to a greater extent intelligence. The schools have no role to play in these traits.

Environmental Traits.

Our surroundings also determine our personality. Some of the beliefs, values, and attitudes are environmental. If the environment in and around is not conducive, there is a negative and poor quality of people, we tend to become so. People are not hard working, honest and sincere, we also adapt to the same and adjust with the new environment or otherwise.

Scope of Personality Development in Residential Schools.

Holistic Personality Development is the first and foremost objective of a Residential School. As the parents do everything to groom their children at home, the schools do much more particularly the residential ones. Besides sending their wards to schools, parents arrange tuitions and coaching. Make them join clubs, gyms, games, music etc. The Residential Schools have all this with them. The following aspects of Residential School shape the Personality of the Children.

The Culture and Traditions.

Residential Schools have a unique culture. They have both home as well as school culture. As it is always said that children imbibe good values and good habits at home and get education in school. Family is the first school where the child gets informal education and goes to school for formal education. But Residential School is both a family and school. Therefore, there is good scope for the development of all personality traits. In fact, personality development is the tradition in Residential School.

Enhancing Knowledge, Skills and Attitude of the Students.

Residential Schools focus on improving the knowledge of students, develop core skills particularly the soft skills and make them positive to self and others. **Inventive, innovative and interactive teaching learning strategies make them intelligent, diligent and positive.** The teachers and students are always updated with the latest developments taking place in and around.the culture and tradition is such that they get several opportunities to develop all domains of their personality.

Initiate Maximum Participation.

Residential Schools do not only organise a variety of activities but also invite maximum participation. It is compulsory for every student to choose one or the other activity, prepare thoroughly and excel in it. There are morning PT exercises, games and sports for physical development and literary and scientific activities for mental growth. Scope for building good relationships, sharing and caring with each other and for each other strengthen their emotional domain.

Cordial and Conducive Environment.

The overall environment of a Residential School is by and large conducive. It is homely and friendly. Students enjoy freedom but within limit under the guardianship and supervision of their teachers. In the regulatory environment there is very little scope for any act of indiscipline. Indiscipline in any form among the students or teachers adversely affects personality development. Such incidents rather create a negative personality which is harmful for self and others.

Residential Schools initiate several personality development programs. Every activity may it be scholastic or co-scholastic, any activity is meant for physical, mental, moral, emotional and spiritual development of students. Schools provide sufficient facilities and ample opportunities for personality development.

CHAPTER XII

Morning Assembly

"The fruit of silence is prayer.
The fruit of prayer is faith.
The fruit of faith is love.
The fruit of love is service.
Our service is for the poorest of the poor."
Mother Teresa

Morning Assembly begins with seeking the love and blessings of the Almighty, and to start the day's work on an optimistic note with a clear and pristine mind. It is the best platform for the Principal, teachers and students to be together at one place to stand, sing a prayer and seek blessings. It sets the tone for the entire day.

OBJECTIVES

To invoke the blessing of the Almighty for successfully doing our day's work

To internalize the essence of prayer and noble thoughts.

To inculcate the values of punctuality, regularity, sincerity, and discipline among students and staff of the vidyalaya.

To be aware of the events taking place in the country & abroad.

To instill self-confidence and a sense of belongingness among the staff and students.

To keep abreast with the latest developments.

To promote feelings of patriotism and national integration among students and staff.

To unfold, promote, and exhibit talent and creativity.

To develop a sense of responsibility and leadership qualities among students and staff.

To give necessary instruction/information to students.

STRENGTHS

1. **Unifies the School**

   ○ Staff & students assemble together.
   ○ Develops a feeling of oneness.
   ○ Opportunity to share experiences & ideas.
   ○ Develops a sense of belongingness & identity.

2. **Promotes Moral Values**

   ○ Spirituality.
   ○ Personal & social values.
   ○ Discipline.
   ○ Punctuality.
   ○ Sincerity.
   ○ Responsibility.

Develops Self-Expression

- ○ Confidence.
  ○ Communication.
  ○ Listening.
  ○ Empathy.
  ○ Appreciation.
  ○ Recognition of achievements of students & teachers.
  ○ Highlighting special achievements of the vidyalaya.
  ○ Motivation of students to exhibit their talent/ creativity.

- Developing respect for others.
- Giving information/instruction.
- Enables to preserve, protect & propagate healthy traditions/practices, culture, and thoughts.
- Helps in building a healthy environment in school.
- Tones up the academic climate of the school.
- Provides a platform to share current news & views.

WEAKNESSES

1. Lack of punctuality & interest for participation.
2. Harsh weather conditions and inadequate infrastructural facilities mar proper conduct of assembly in some vidyalayas.
3. Lack of time management in the conduct of the assembly.
4. Lack of guidance for planning, preparation.
5. Limitations of the music teacher being either a vocalist or an instrumentalist.
6. Lack of stamina in some students.

REMEDIES

1. Principal to become a role model.
2. Providing required infrastructure & facilities.
3. Keeping time for each activity to conclude in the stipulated time of 20 minutes.
4. All teachers, especially Music, Language teachers & PETs, play an anchor role.
5. Variety of activities to arouse interest amongst students, such as displaying paintings of the week, news on inventions/discoveries, projects, models, innovation guest lectures, etc., should also be included.

6. To define & articulate the importance of morning assembly to develop interest & voluntary participation.
7. Training inputs for playing various musical instruments by music teachers .
8. Compilation of quiz questions, thoughts, and moral talks as a knowledge treasure.
9. Presence of a staff nurse in the assembly to attend to any case of indisposition.

Suggested ACTIVITIES OF ASSEMBLY PROGRAMME

1. Roll call (House wise/class wise) - 3 min.
2. Prayer - 4 min.
3. Pledge - 2 min.
4. Thought for the Day - 1 min.
5. News Headlines (International, National, Local, Sports, Inventions, etc.) - 3 min.
6. Meditation - 2 min.
7. Student talk (Book review/Quiz/Poetry, etc.) - 2 min.
8. Address by Teacher/MOD/Principal - 2 min.
9. National Anthem - 1 min. (52 sec.)

Total time taken for the conduct of assembly: 20 min.

Note: It is desirable to conduct the assembly in all three languages ie English, Hindi and Regional Language on alternate basis.

CHAPTER XIII

Where Teaching Is a Mission

"A good education can change anyone,
A good teacher can change everyone"

Residential School Teachers are not simply teachers or professionals, they are rather Missionaries. They understand that the students are with them throughout the school days and therefore, teaching responsibilities are somehow different from other schools. They are busy during school hours and busier after the school hours. They have to help the gifted and guide the underachievers. Their teaching styles and strategies are very effective, innovative and interactive. Simultaneously they play the role of parents as well. Teaching with enthusiasm, zeal and spirit are the main mantras of teachers.

The teachers in Residential Schools are a very busy community rather the busiest of all. But they are groomed in such a way that they hardly feel stressed and over-burdened. The simple thing they follow is

If you worry you can't work.

If you work, you need not to worry.

Residential Schools are known for quality education which is the outcome of Effective Teaching Learning Strategies. Achieving quality results through the meritorious students and a team of competent and committed teachers realize the objective of **Academic Excellence.** The following are the teaching strategies adopted by the teachers in most of the Residential

Schools....

Planning, Preparation and Presentation.

Planning is an integral component of teaching. It is not mere lesson planning or Dairy Planning. It is rather a systematic planning to make the lesson interesting, joyful and comprehendible. It includes planning of contents, methods and activities.

Preparation is to be ready to deliver the planned content. A well-prepared teacher can only justify the teaching learning process.

Presentation is the method of delivery. The teacher may follow different methods in accordance with the difficulty level of content and level of students.

Inventive, Innovative and Interactive Strategies.

Invention is to introduce some newness, explore **new** methodology, activities. Innovation is to apply the inventions. Interaction is to actively involve the students and invite their participation.

Transmission, Transaction and Transformation.

Transmission is whatever useful the teacher delivers in the class. It is imparting some information and developing skills. Transaction is bipolar teaching learning i.e. not only the teacher is active but the students are also active. Transformation is to bring a desirable change in behavior i.e. entry behavior and terminal behavior. Whatever the students already know about the content being taught and what they have learnt after the transmission and transaction.

Effective Communication Strategies.

Teacher is expected to be the best communicator. Learning depends on how the subject matter has been communicated. Communication is not only speaking, reading and writing. It is much more than this. Teachers must be competent enough to communicate verbally as well as Non-Verbally. **Verbal Communication includes**

The way the teacher speaks. Whatever the teacher communicates should be clear, understandable and comprehensible. It is the communication in words, lecture, demonstration, discussions, messages etc.

The way the teacher writes. Must be written in neat, clean and legible handwriting.

Voice and Pitch of the teacher has to be moderate. Clear voice facilitates learning. The pitch should neither be very low nor very high.

Non-verbal Communication is in terms of facial expressions, body language, gestures, postures, eye contact etc.

Many things can be communicated through facial expressions such as conveying yes or no through nods, neck movements.

Gestures... This type of communication is through the teacher's body parts, hands, face, eyes, pointing towards an object, indicating excellent, poor with fingers, which can be seen and noticed by the students.

Postures... This is the positioning of the teacher's body ie the way the teacher stands, sits, moves, bends in the class. Children very carefully notice these posture and enjoy the undesirable postures.

Eye Contact... This to establish rapport through eyes. Teachers must look into the eyes of students in order to invite their attention and involve them in the learning process. Eye contact doesn't mean staring and making them worried. This contact should be only for a few seconds.

'Students are not generally very good at listening to their elders but never forget to imitate their behavior and actions'.

Teachers of Residential Schools spend more time with students, non-verbal communication is a regular exercise.

Activity Oriented Teaching.

When I listen, I forget.

When I see it I remember.

When I do I understand.

The focus of an effective teacher is always understanding. To make the students learn and understand, teaching through various content related activities is of great help. Activities not only make the teaching a joyful event but also facilitate learning, making them retain and recollect the contents taught. There can be both students and teacher related activities.

Maximum use of black/white board, drawing, practicals, story-telling, demonstration, field visits etc. can be some teacher related activities. Reading, writing, speaking, group exercises, role playing etc. are some of the activities in which the students can be involved.

Pragmatic and not Dogmatic Strategies.

Residential Schools are often serious towards the professional growth of teachers. The teachers are always updated and equipped. Their approach is pragmatic. Pragmatic strategies are experience and practical based. The teachers facilitate learning through life experiences and experiments rather than simply narrating and explaining. On the other hand, Dogmatic strategies are outdated, conventional and obsolete.

Conceptual and not Procedural Teaching. Real teaching is not to follow the procedure i.e. going to class, write something on board, explain and walk off. It is procedural Teaching. Conceptual Teaching is to focus on concepts, concept clearance and removal of doubts.

Prepared and not experienced teacher.

Residential School teachers don't go to the class as experienced teachers but go as prepared teachers. A good teacher is one who thoroughly prepares the content to be taught. They are always prepared to face the challenges thrown by the students.

Taking care of Must be taught, Should be Taught and Could be Taught Syllabus

(M-S-C) areas.

Must be taught content which is prescribed in the syllabus, is very important from an examination point of view and about which the principal, students and parents are seriously concerned. **Should be taught content** is going beyond the textbooks, syllabus and giving additional information. It may enrich the students to score more. **Could be taught** is the content which may not be exams oriented but may be important in life. It is also known as Hidden Curriculum.

Learner Centred Strategies.

It is not very important what has been taught but most important is what has been learnt. Now the learner is in the centre of the entire teaching learning process. The new education policy aims at a learner friendly environment and therefore, there is...

Learner friendly curriculum

Learner friendly textbooks

Learner friendly teaching

Learner friendly policy

So the teacher should also follow a learner friendly teaching methodology. In a Residential School the Learners are in close contact with their teachers. The teachers make every effort to make them learn. Therefore, the learner centred strategies yield good results.

The learners are often of three type:

High achievers or gifted.

Average.

Underachievers.

In simple words we can call them as.

Can do learners.

Don't do learners.

Can't do learners.

Can do... are high scorers. They are so talented that even without the help of teachers they can perform much better. Teachers' assistance will further enrich and equip them. The number of these learners is generally less in class.

Don't do... are the learners who can do but may be because of carelessness or diverted attention they don't perform better. They are physically in the class but mentally somewhere else. The number of such students can be more in the class.

Can't do... learners are not able to perform despite all efforts. They remain under achievers. Remedial teaching is required for this type of students.

In Residential School the teachers are very well aware of all types of learners. They plan the teaching learning strategies accordingly.

Although excellence is the Mission of every Residential School yet Academic excellence is one of the important objectives. The Residential Schools with the help of a team of dedicated principals and teachers are successful in accomplishing the objectives.

CHAPTER XIV

Self and Supervised Studies

"God helps those who help themselves"

One of the important features of a Residential School is conduct of Supervised studies. A considerable time is allotted for this in the Daily Routine. As at home the children are under the supervision of their parents, in school their teachers are the supervisors. This is not much different from self-studies. In self-studies there may not be any assistance, the students have to help themselves. Even at home the parents don't have so much time to sit with children, supervise and guide them. They may be in a position to help the tiny tots but they may not be able to help the children at every level. However, in a Residential School this is not only made possible but it is rather obligatory on the part of every teacher to guide the students and clear their doubts. That is why Supervised Studies is an integral component and one of the subsystems of Residential School.

We can very well understand the concept of supervised studies. The phrase is self- explanatory. It is known as 'Supervised' because the teachers are the supervisors. It is conducted under the close vigil and supervision of teachers. The supervision duties are allotted keeping in view the need, discipline and support. Therefore, a mixed group of subject teachers, MOD, PTI numbering four to five is put on duty. They supervise, ensure silence, make them attentive and guide and help if need be. They do not only mind them but also encourage them to complete the assigned tasks. It is in fact shifting from the formal teaching learning in the classes to a supervised self-study system.

Objectives.

Develop self-study habits.

The purpose is to make them responsible for themselves. In the beginning when the child is admitted, he/she may not be aware of this system of study. At home it is not so organized and systematic. Gradually they become habitual of this and it becomes a habit.

Completion of Assigned Tasks.

As the schedule in Residential School is very tight, this is the only time at the disposal of students to complete the assigned works i.e. Home-work, projects, assignments etc.

Peer learning and peer tutoring.

It is always useful when students help each other in learning. Sometimes peer tutoring and peer learning becomes more advantageous than classroom teaching. A high achiever may be more helpful to guide the underachiever than a teacher.

Improve Performance.

Parents, teachers and students themselves want continuous and consistent improvement in performance. Sometimes the students may not be very attentive in their classes. They lack behind and fail to score good marks. The supervised studies provide them an opportunity to revise the content taught, take the help of teachers and improve their understanding. Some of the teachers also take extra classes during this period.

Strengthen Value base.

Supervised studies imbibe many values in students. As this is a regular feature of every Residential School, the students report on time, revise their courses, complete their assignments and help each other. They learn the importance of punctuality, regularity, sincerity, seriousness cooperation and become self responsible and self dependent.

Keeping Gainfully Engaged.

The purpose of conducting Supervised Studies is also to keep the students engaged in gainful activities. In case they are not engaged and supervised, they may create any nuisance and hamper the smooth functioning of the school. It is therefore essential to keep them engaged under the supervision and observation of their teachers.

Time Management.

Time is very precious. Almost all subsystems of Residential School teach the students the importance of time and its effective management. Every activity in school is time bound and has to be undertaken within the time allotted for it. Similarly from supervised studies, students also learn proper utilization of time.

Features of supervised studies.

This being an important aspect of Residential School, must be taken seriously and sincerely. Both teacher and taught need to be particular while attempting this exercise. Some of the features are as under

Good supervised Studies are **effective and impressive.**

Arouse interest in students towards self-studies and make them self-dependent.

Inculcate a sense of discipline as the students study in a guided and regulated environment.

Teachers support Facilitates the learning.

Calm and quiet atmosphere is created.

Creates cordial and conducive learning environment.

Aims at improving the focus, attention and concentration of students.

Effective supervision motivates and boosts the morale of students.

Attracts the students towards their strengths and weaknesses.

CHAPTER XV

Diagnostic, Remedial and Enrichment Teaching

"I love to learn but hate to be taught

Winston Churchill"

One of the unique features of Residential Schools is to assist to monitor the performance of students on a regular basis. The group of students in classes is never homogeneous; it is rather heterogeneous. In regular class the teacher proceeds at his own pace. Some of the students are so bright that this teaching is average for them. Whereas some are not that good and the teaching goes beyond their heads. Residential school has to monitor the achievements of all the students as it is their earnest responsibility. **Therefore, think tanks in education have propounded a unique Teaching Learning system known as Diagnostic, Remedial and Enrichment Teaching.**

Diagnostic Process.

As in medical science diagnosis is to find the cause of sickness on the basis of symptoms, in education too the reasons for underachievement are identified, analysed and remedy is planned. Diagnostic process helps the teachers to chalk down their strategies to help the students whose pace of learning is comparatively slower than the peers. Their learning gaps/ difficulties are identified in this process. Various tools and techniques can be adopted in the diagnostic process...

Testing Techniques.

Simple and easiest possible tests in the concerned subject can be administered and performance is assessed. On the basis of scores the teachers can know the weaknesses i.e. failing to explain, lacking in knowledge, skills, understanding, writing speed etc. Accordingly, the remedy can be planned.

Observation Techniques.

Teachers are the keen observers. By observing the following they can diagnose the learning problems...

Responses.

When questions are raised by the teacher, some of the students are not able to respond or their responses are not satisfactory. They don't raise any questions.

Participation.

Some of them do not participate in the teaching learning process. Neither interact nor take interest. Teachers can easily know that they are not understanding.

Body Language.

Teachers can observe the body language of the students. Their gestures, postures, eye contact nods also show that they are learning or not.

Attention.

Some of the students are not attentive in the class. Their attention is somehow diverted. They may be physically in the class and mentally somewhere else. It indicates that they are not learning.

Attendance.

One of the reasons for underachievement is absence from classes. Those who remain absent on one or the other pretext, remain behind the peers and identified as slow learners.

Passive Listening.

Students who do not actively listen to their teachers are left behind. Active listening is as important as other learning tools.

Checking the entry and terminal behavior.

Entry behaviour is what the child already knows or the previous knowledge. Terminal behaviour is what the child has learnt after the delivery by the teacher. If there's no considerable change, it means that the child is either not learning or has learnt very little.

The diagnostic techniques may yield the following results

They may be slow at learning because of:

Lack of knowledge and set of skills.

Poor understanding

Less grasping power

Not attentive,

Non adjustment.

Slow writing Speed.

Low on Confidence.

Remedial Teaching.

After having done the diagnosis, well planned and systematic Remedial strategies are required. Remedial Teaching is to address the problems of learners on one-to-one basis as well as in group. It is not routine teaching. It is a specialized form of teaching and undertaken after school hours. It is subject wise. Teachers devote extra time for this. There is very little scope for such a type of teaching in day schools. But it is invariably conducted in Residential Schools where the teachers and students are available every time.

Remedial teaching needs to be conducted seriously and sincerely because it deals with a different group of students who are not only slow at learning but may also be careless, naughty, undisciplined, arrogant and least bothered. While dealing with them the teacher has to keep in mind that it is not the child who is to be criticized for failure but the behaviour which is responsible. Criticizing the child is a futile exercise which lowers his self-esteem and the pace of learning will further decline.

It is also known as Selective Teaching. The following techniques can be helpful in remediation.

Selective Package.

Remediation is neither extra class nor re teaching of the content already taught. Underachievers are not in a position to grasp the entire syllabus of a particular subject. Therefore, the teacher has to prepare a package consisting of the easy portion from every unit. The identified students may be asked to comprehend and master this only. Their testing, retesting will be out of this only. It should also be thoroughly revised. The students will not feel overburdened, take interest and score better.

Capsule program.

This is a specific teaching program prepared in some topics of the subject which is important from examination point of view. It doesn't include all units as in selective units but only a small portion of syllabus e.g. fifty present or so. The students are asked to learn by heart, repeat, revise and retain so that they can score at least pass marks. This type of capsule is very useful for board class students. It has been experimented in many schools and yielded desirable results.

Special Attention.

One of the reasons for underachievement is non attention by some students in class. Though the teacher is required to pay attention to all students and involve them in the teaching learning process yet, in the class of a larger group individual attention becomes difficult. In Remedial class the group may reduce to one fourth even. Therefore, one to one attention and removal of their doubts is possible.

Motivation.

Such a set of students need morale boosting from time to time. Upper hand of the teacher, encouragement and support is essential.

Practice Learning by Writing.

When I listen I forget.

When I see I member

When I do I understand.

As discussed above the students slow at writing speed are not able to cope up with others. In exams they cannot attempt all questions and achieve less marks, hence identified as underachievers and need remediation. They must be exposed to learning by writing methods in class, during self and supervised studies. It will not only improve their speed but also spellings, understanding and sentence formation.

Enrichment Teaching.

In every school there are gifted students also. Their number may be small. Such a set of students are not much benefitted in general classroom teaching. They need something additional and special. They need to be enriched and equipped with additional knowledge, skills and information. Therefore, Enrichment Teaching is meant for such students. Residential Schools are known for their enrichment programs and therefore, the students excel. There is provision to provide special impetus to these students.

Enrichment is value addition i.e. enhancing quality and degree of excellence by providing additional inputs

in terms of standardized teaching. It can be self enrichment as well as enrichment by teachers. Gifted are competent enough to enrich and equip themselves by their rigorous studies, gathering additional subject related information and by being attentive in the class. But the best sources are their teachers who are their guides, guardians and mentors.

The first and foremost requirement of enrichment is the enriched and suitably equipped teachers. To provide enrichment teachers must be abreast with latest information, new knowledge, researches, innovations and experimentations in the subject. Inadequate knowledge, ineffective teaching, dogmatic methodology cannot help enrichment.

Some of the suggestive enrichment strategies are
Special packages with quality material.

Assignments and Projects to acquire additional knowledge and skills.

Inventive innovative and interactive teaching learning strategies.

Tutorials.

Intensive guidance provided to a set of students.

Extensive Learning.

This to help in acquiring new knowledge and understanding.

Involving in critical thinking, creativity, reasoning, problem solving.

Going beyond the syllabus and textbooks.

Mentoring.

Helping, guiding and supporting.

Computer Assisted Learning, Technological tools, AI.

CHAPTER XVI

Value Based Education

"Values can not be taught but are caught"

It is often said that the child gets education in school and values in the family. **Family is the first school.** But residential school is both a school and a family. Therefore, the responsibility of Residential School is not only to provide Quality Education but also imbibe good values in students. The system of Residential School is such that values automatically filter downwards from teacher to taught.

WHAT IS VALUE?

- Quality of being useful or important.
- Beliefs about what is wrong or right.
- Values are formed early in life.
- Values do get challenged as we grow.

FUNDAMENTAL VALUES FROM RELIGION.

Every Religion preaches the following universal or fundamental values. These are common values in all faiths and beliefs.

- Truth
- Love
- Peace
- Non-violence
- Righteous conduct

ROLE OF SCHOOLS IN VALUE-BASED EDUCATION

- Schools should prepare a comprehensive program for value-based education.
- Efforts should be made to imbibe values through morning assemblies, scholastic, and co-scholastic activities.

VARIOUS VALUEs specifically developed in **Residential Schools.**
PHYSICAL VALUES

- Healthy body
- Stoutness
- Appropriateness
- Beauty
- Handsomeness

The rigorous physical exercises, participation in various games and sports keep the children physically fit, healthy, smart and good looking.
PERSONAL VALUES

- Self-confidence
- Self-reliance
- Satisfaction
- Patience
- Humour
- Kindness
- Simplicity

The Residential System promotes the philosophy of 'simple living and high thinking'. The culture of the system is such that the students become self dependent, helping, generous and empathetic.

ECONOMIC VALUES

- Income by fair means
- Useful donations
- Judicious spending

They learn the lessons of honesty, integrity and proper utilization of money.

MORAL VALUES

- Honesty
- Integrity
- Sincerity
- Belongingness

Residential Schools not only prepare a physically fit and mentally alert child but also morally sound student.

SOCIAL VALUES

- Sympathy
- Empathy
- Humanity
- Cooperation

The students are so close and related to each other that they help each other, cooperate and coordinate.

POLITICAL VALUES

- Patriotism
- Freedom
- Democratic outlook

- Discipline

These values are developed through morning assembly, house system and various curricular and cocurricular activities.

RELIGIOUS VALUES

- Faith
- Divinity
- Worship

The children believe in different faiths, free to worship their god, offer prayers and seek blessings.

INTELLECTUAL VALUES

- Imagination
- Creativity
- Understanding
- Problem-solving
- Decision-making

Excellent and effective teaching learning strategies promote the above values.

SCIENTIFIC VALUES

- Scientific temper
- Reasoning
- Logical thinking

Residential Schools endeavor to develop scientific temperament, attitude and thinking.

AESTHETIC VALUES

* Sense of beauty
* Love for art and nature.

The students are brought up in a pure, pollution free, scenic and lush green environment. Their aesthetic sense automatically develops.

SPIRITUAL VALUES

* Self-awareness
* Consciousness
* Meditation

Students are exposed to various yogic exercises, taught to meditate and realize self.

Residential Schools provide the best opportunities and an appropriate platform for value-based education. Their value system becomes so strong that they succeed in every endeavor of their lives. They come out to be the best professionals, entrepreneurs, leaders and on the top of it aware citizens of the nation. **Students continue to uphold the values cherished by the school throughout their lives.**

CHAPTER XVII

The Principal A Father Figure

"As is the Principal, so is the School. The Personality of Principal reflects in the school he/ she heads."

The role of Principal in Residential School is very crucial. It is unlike other schools where the Principals are normally Academic Heads. Here the Principal has multidisciplinary roles. Besides academics the Principal has to oversee the hostels, mess, safety and security, well being, procurement, finances and many other areas. Therefore, multidimensional roles can be played only by a multifarious personality. The Principal is the leader of the Institution, an Institutional Head. Must lead by examples and not by rhetoric. The Residential Schools therefore, appoint the incumbent as Principal who possesses meritorious academic qualifications, desirable residential experience, managerial, administrative and leadership skills.

Principal is the 'Father Figure' in the institution. He/ She is the 'Foster Parent' of students and staff, a Guardian and a Guide. He is the person who builds healthy relations and develops **belongingness. Principal therefore, discharges** the parental duties and responsibilities which the parents perform at home. **Therefore, the school becomes a home but away from home.**

Various roles played by the Principal can be summarized as under.

An Academician.

Though Excellence is the foremost objective of a Residential School yet it is an academic acumenship of the Principal that motivates, and guides the teachers and students to achieve the best results.

An Administrator

There are a number of administrative tasks to be performed by the Principal in a Residential School. Maintaining discipline amongst the staff and students is perhaps the most crucial one. It is in fact twenty four hour task. Besides, safety and security, personnel administration, financial administration are some other administrative responsibilities.

A Manager

As a manager the Principal has to manage a number of areas. Mess management, financial management, resource management, office management are some of the aspects. Effective management depends on the managerial and soft skills of the Principal.

A Leader.

'Your Vision has brought us this far, your inspiration will take us further'

Leader not only leads but sets examples and becomes a role model. Leader is one who has a vision and a mission. This vision becomes a shared vision as the teachers and students scrupulously follow it to accomplish the objectives.

> *"Most people think leadership as a Position and therefore don't see themselves as good leaders."*
> *Stephen Covey*

Above all - A Human Being.

Besides an Academician, Administrator, Manager and a Leader, a Principal is a person who is there all the time, a fatherly figure, a guardian. All above roles have Positional Power, an Authority. But the most important power is the Personal Power. In a **Residential School, an effective and competent Principal uses more of his Personal power than the Positional Power.**

Qualities of a good Principal of Residential Schools

Knowledge, skills and Attitude.

'Knowledge decides what to say.

Skill decides how to say.

Attitude decides how much to say.

Wisdom decides whether to say or not'.

These are the essential requirements of any job to be performed effectively. Without having sufficient knowledge of Residential system, lack of skill sets and willingness to perform, principal cannot succeed. Therefore, the Principal of a Residential School must possess the essential and desirable knowledge. Hard as well as soft skills and positive Attitude.

As is the Principal, so is the School. The personality of a Principal reflects in the Institution he/she heads. The achievements of the school both in scholastic and co-scholastic spheres depend on the managerial and leadership skills of the Principal.

Principal is the Wall Mirror for the staff and students. Principal guides, motivates, decides, delegates and therefore, the most responsible person in the Institution. Good Principal is always goal oriented rather than rule oriented.

All stakeholders very closely observe the walk, talk, behavior action and accent of the Principal. Therefore, one has to be very particular and vigilant in this regard.

Principal is an Institution in himself/herself.

The Dress and Address of the Principal is of paramount importance. Smartly dressed up principal leaves an impact on all. The teachers and students are very much impressed by this attribute. The approach of the Principal should be people centric for regeneration and rejuvenation. Thus, the Principal of a Residential School is expected to wear many hats.

Principal must have the principles of integrity, honesty, sincerity, morality, truthfulness, justice and impartiality.

A man of words, true to his words. What is said by the Principal doesn't matter but how it is said is very Important. The tone, pitch, language used matters a lot.

Must be available easily to all. Must not expect the people to come to you, try to go to them. Must come out of walls and think out of the box. Think first and talk later.

Problem solving skills and an Analytical Mind. Should be able to mitigate risks. Has to be a good crisis manager. Silly mistakes may cause a problem. Needs to be solved amicably. Should not involve in fault finding business. It is perhaps the easiest job.

'What is the most difficult and most easy thing in life? Answer,' MISTAKES.

"Very easy to judge when others do it and very difficult to realize when we do it."

APJ Kalam

Demanding and a Commanding Person. Driven by the vision of the Organization. Trust the team and become Trustworthy. **Trust is the most expensive thing in the world. It can take years to earn but only a few seconds to lose.**

Remember five things you can not recover

A stone after it is thrown.

A word after it is said.

An opportunity after it is missed.

Time after it is gone.

Trust after it is lost.

Excellent Communication skills both verbal and written. Must be able to communicate in a simple language, clear voice and without showing any temperament. Must not mince words while talking.

A Person of Decisions and Actions.

'Quick decisions are unsafe decisions'.

The decisions taken have to be fair, judicious and impartial. The actions shouldn't be hurting and damaging.

'I am not a product of my circumstances, I am the product of my decisions'. Actions shouldn't be for letting the people down but for lifting them up.

Stephen Covey.

Personal and Professional Effectiveness.

The Principal of a Residential School is expected to be an effective person as well as an effective professional. Must be able to impress and influence the stakeholders by the ways of his/her functioning during the stint and leave an impact and legacy behind when not there.

Strong Interpersonal Relations.

'Relations shine by shaking hands in the best moments but they blossom by holding hands in critical moments'.

Functioning of Residential School is twenty-four hours and all are actively engaged in one or the other works. All are very close to each other, meet everyday and interact. In such an environment any threat to Interpersonal relations will adversely affect the entire system. The Principal is the right person to build healthy relations, strengthen them and keep them intact.

Maturity.

'Your words may express your thoughts but your efforts represent you:.

Principal is supposed to be the most mature person in the school. Being a head, a leader and a guardian maturity must be reflected in every walk, talk, behaviour, action and attire. All stakeholders look at the Principal for the possible solution of their grievances hence maturity is always noticeable. **Principal on every occasion must display maturity and patience and not be swayed by hearsay or speculative reports.**

Healthy lifestyle.

'It is not important how long we live but most important is how well we live'.

The Principal of a Residential School is perhaps the busiest person in the system. Everybody looks towards him for everything. Therefore, a lot of energy is required. In order to accumulate this energy, a healthy lifestyle is very essential.

The affable attitude of the Principal, close association with the staff and students, sincere guardianship and timely motivation gives them strength and moral support . They love to live, learn and serve the Institution, feel at home and the **School becomes a Home Away from Home.**

Transparency and Impartiality.

Principal must have a transparent approach. Should be open minded. The team being headed should not be kept in any sort of suspense. Everything should be crystal clear and noticeable. Partiality in administration is always dangerous. It discourages and disappoints the people and their zeal and spirit to perform is adversely affected.

Team Spirit.

'Alone I can say but together we can talk, alone I can enjoy but together we can celebrate, alone I can smile but together we can laugh'.

Although Working with a team, infusing team spirit and improving it is an important Leadership function yet in Residential school where the task of every team member is very challenging, Team Concept becomes more relevant and significant. Principal therefore, must be competent enough to form suitable teams, assign them work and get it successfully accomplished.

Principal of a Residential School is the person who can help in upholding the rich traditions and culture of the school, facilitate the adjustment and adaptation of students and teachers. **Being a Father Figure in the school, can truly convert the school into a Home.**

CHAPTER XVIII

Role of Teachers Friends, Guides and Guardians

*"A Station Master minds the Trains, a School
Master Trains the Minds*

Dr. Radhakrishnan."

Teacher is a friend, a Philosopher and a Guide. This applies in all educational institutions but is very relevant to Residential schools. In a normal school system the teacher may not find time to guide the students after school hours. But the Residential School job is full time. The teachers not only teach but perform the responsibilities of parents and guardians.. The residential system of schools has been inherited from the ancient Gurukul System where the teachers were the GURUS. **Guru is a Sanskrit word which means "Darkness to Brightness."** And this clearly defines the role of teacher.

Teachers are not born but teachers are made. Teacher can not teach unless he himself/herself keeps learning. **They should be subject wizards.**

'A lamp cannot light another lamp unless it is still **burning its own flame'**

RN Tagore

Teacher is like a burning candle , it consumes itself to light the way for others .

In the Gurukul System Guru was worshipped as God, sometimes above God.

हरि रूठे गुरु ठौर है, गुरु रूठे नहीं ठौर

In Indian culture, a teacher is the only person compared with God. Performs all three functions of God, Creation, preservation and destruction. Makes students fit to face challenges, creates values in them. Preserves the essential goodness of learning, musters the strength to overcome the evils and destroys all negativity. Our scholars have composed several lines for gurus.

गुरु गोविदि दोनों खड़े, काके लागूं पाय,

बलिहारी गुरु आपने गोविदि दयो बताय।

गुरु देवो गुरु धर्मो, गुरु निष्ठा परंतप:,

गुरु परातरं नास्ति, भबिरहुम कथयता।

गुरुब्रह्मा गुरुर्विष्णु: गुरुर्देवो महेश्वर:।

गुरु साक्षात् पर:ब्रह्म तस्मै श्रीगुरवे नम:।

Guru guides to walk through the path of perfection, teacher introduces the students to the external world, Guru to the internal world i.e. to realize self.

This is what a teacher does. Takes the students from darkness of ignorance to the brightness of knowledge, enlightenment. Teachers of Residential Schools are not simply teachers but they are the **GURUS, the MASTERS.** In eminent Residential Schools faculty members are not called teachers, they are known as Masters. Even the head is not known as Principal but as a Headmaster. **Masters are the specialists, experts, transformers, reformers. They therefore, are not only the Masters but the 'Mastros'.**

Three roles of Guru:

- **To protect and nourish.**
- **To teach and correct**
- **To guide the disciple's ideas and conduct.**

We can draw a distinction between teacher and a master...

- Teacher gives information whereas Master transforms.
- Teachers dealswith knowledge, makes students intelligent. Master takes from intelligence to wisdom.
- Teacher basically deals with our exterior. Master strengthens our interior.
- Every master is a teacher but every teacher may not be a Master.

Teachers in Residential Schools are the real champions. They are masters in every field who can teach, preach, guide, motivate, inspire, imbibe values and build character. They are Nation Builders as well as Institution Builders. A teacher of a Residential School is a Fighter. **'Has never give up Attitude'.**

Teaching is the profession of teaching other professions. It is the profession of professions.

Role of Teacher in Residential School.

Teacher's role in Residential School is very challenging, result oriented and multifunctional. Teacher is a demonstrator, a dispenser of Information, a taskmaster, role model, inspirer, surrogate parent, a therapist, an evangelist, a persuader, a propagandist, a stimulator of inquiry and many others. Teachers are the kingpin in the educational system. But in the Residential system the expectations from teachers are tremendous. Besides effective teachers they are expected to be the parents, guardians and guides of students. Teachers engage the students in creative pursuits.

An Academician.

One who opts teaching must not cease learning. Only an excellent teacher can produce excellent results. Residential School teachers never fail in their academic accomplishments. They are always aware of the latest teaching tools and techniques. They are fully prepared.

A House Master.

In Residential School the house masters are selected out of the competent, experienced and committed teachers. This role is more challenging than that of a teacher. House master is an administrator as well as a manager. He/she is the most respected, wanted and beloved of students.

A Parent, Guardian and Guide.

Students are at the disposal of their teachers in Residential School. The social and emotional needs of students are fulfilled by their teachers. They are not the real parents but of course not less than them. They take every care of them and provide desired love and affection. They are the pastoral or loco parents. They are their guardians who guide them, give advice, stop them from any wrong deeds and motivate them for their betterment.

Qualities of a Residential School Teacher.
Academic Qualities.

Every School appoints the teachers on the basis of their educational qualifications essential for the job. But in a Residential School besides the essential academic qualifications the teacher must possess certain desirable abilities such as determination, commitment and confidence. Must possess thorough knowledge of the subject, teaching skills and methods. Obsolete and dogmatic methods must be done away with. Must enrich and enhance knowledge by updating with latest developments that have taken place in the subject. Has to be **A constant Learner.** Children in the new millennium need to develop a spirit of inquiry which makes learning a joyful activity. There is a dire need to redefine the traditional role of teacher from an Instructor to a Facilitator. Child is the Master of Learning. Teachers must remember that 'Nothing can be Taught but Everything can be Learned'. Residential School Teacher is the Teacher by Choice and not by Chance.

Remember

A poor teacher tells,

An average teacher explains,

A good teacher demonstrates,

But a Great Teacher Inspires.

Professional Qualities.

Teaching profession requires many other abilities and competencies besides academic qualifications. In a Residential School teaching is not merely a profession, it is rather a Mission. Professional qualities include proper training, skills, experience, teaching aptitude and attitude. The willingness for the profession and belongingness to it are very essential.

Technology is the need of hour. Teachers must be technology savvy. It has now entered every classroom. The teachers have to be sufficiently proficient in using it. It is also said that time is ahead when teachers will be replaced by teaching machines. But it is a myth. It is only the teacher whose presence is felt, who can make learning vibrant, authentic and interactive.

Personality Traits.

'Let your work speak for your personality. Never look at your profession as drudgery'.

Students are influenced by the personality of their teachers. A smartly dressed, physically strong, intelligent and well-spoken teacher leaves an ever lasting impact.

Teachers must not shirk from responsibility, character should be one's biggest asset. **Residential school teacher needs to be a worker not a shirker.**

Disciplinary Qualities.

Teacher has to be a strict disciplinarian. Self-discipline is an emergent requirement of the teaching profession in general and for a Residential School teacher in particular. Teacher who himself is not disciplined can never maintain discipline in the class. Students are inspired by his/her good subject knowledge and teaching skills.

Human Qualities.

Teacher is expected to be a nice human being. Has to be good to self and others. All other qualities Will be of no use if one has no acceptability in the system. Sincerity, honesty, consideration, simplicity, truthfulness, generosity, and smile are some of the essential human qualities of a Residential School Teacher.

Love and kindness are never wasted, they always make a difference'.

Behavioral Qualities.

'Behavior is the mirror of Personality'.

'Behaviour is always greater than knowledge because in life there are many situations where knowledge fails but behavior succeeds'.

Because of the vast and varied roles of a Teacher of Residential School, his/her behavior with the students, fellow colleagues and seniors must be desirable and acceptable. Must have decent behavior and manners. Behavioral traits make the teacher a Role Model. Must not be over critical, a fault finder, short tempered and arrogant. Teacher spends maximum time with students in Presidential School and therefore, has to be humble and docile.

Sound moral character and integrity.

There is an old adage,' **If wealth is lost nothing is lost, if health is lost something is lost, if character is lost**

everything is lost'.

In a Residential School where the teacher is omnipresent, engaged everywhere, needs to demonstrate a sound moral character. It should be beyond doubt.

These qualities of a teacher not only facilitate the learning of students but also help them in their adjustment, keep them happy, satisfied and feel at home. Therefore, a Residential School gradually becomes a Home for them.

CHAPTER XIX

Resilient Parenting

"Without my children, my house would be clean, my wallet will be full but my heart will be empty"

Children are the most precious gifts of god to the parents and parents are irreplaceable entities for children. In the upbringing of children, the most dominating role is of parents. Even if the children are in a boarding school right from the beginning, the role of parents is equally significant. Their love, affection, association and belongingness remain the same wherever their children are. Parents always remain the most loveable, respectable and memorable for them.

There can be several reasons for sending their wards to Residential Schools

Most parents are of the opinion that the residential schools provide the best quality education coupled with holistic personality development. This is true also. Every parent wants to arrange the best education to their wards by curtailing their other expenses.

Maybe the parents are so busy with their businesses, social and political affairs that they don't find much time for the children. The best option is to send them to a boarding school.

Both husband and wife may be working in transferable jobs and posted at distant places. They feel that shifting the children and changing schools adversely affects the studies of their wards. They prefer to admit them in Residential School.

There are instances that the child or the children are beyond the control of parents due to one or the other reasons. Thay find themselves unable to mend their ways. They decide to send them to a Boarding School.

There are some known Residential Schools which are not co-educational. Those are either exclusively girls or boys. Some of the parents do like the Residential set up but don't send children there because of the coeducational system. But they prefer to send to the school which is either for girls or boys only.

There can be many other personal or professional reasons which the parents are not able to encounter and therefore, choose the Residential School for the education of their awards.

After having sent their wards to Residential School the responsibility of parents towards the children does not end. It rather becomes more challenging. Their children may be happy in school but they are always worried and concerned about them, their learning, their living and their well-being. Children of **Residential Schools are shaped by the Hard work of their teachers and Heart work of their parents.**

When the children come home during vacations or breaks, they may need some liberty at home. They have come from a hectic and regulatory environment. They want to be hassle free. Parents may also support their liberty. But it should not be unlimited.

Single child is more difficult to handle. He/she is free from comparison and competition at home. Parents often compare their siblings and have an obvious favorite. The transition to adulthood, rising demands of children for various expensive things and emotional problems are the challenges before most parents. Modern generation children are high on IQ but low on EQ. They are often stressed, lose temper, don't easily follow instructions and are under peer pressure. The children of boarding school may be more demanding at home.

The following suggestive measures if adopted timely and appropriately will certainly help the parents to properly handle and nurture their children ....

"Connection and not correction is the best remedy for every malady." Most parents want to correct their siblings in their own ways. Even the students of Residential School who are with the parents only during holidays follow the same. The parents must establish connection and rapport with the children. Communicating on regular basis, giving them a patient hearing, supporting them are some of the simple strategies yielding good results.

Investing more time than money. Every parent wants to provide the best possible education to their children. This is perhaps one of the reasons for sending them to Boarding School. These days education is the most expensive affair for the parents and they don't mind spending it despite their financial condition. But unfortunately, they don't have time to spend with them and this is the root cause of growing problems of youngsters.

Practice Mindful Parenting. Their emotions must not be hurt in any circumstances. Never over act, over expect and over pamper. It is very difficult for the over pampered child to face the challenges of life. Teach them to meditate. **Meditation is all about dedication and diligence. Make them practice it to realize its physical,** mental and emotional effects. It makes them feel calmer, focused, and attentive. In Residential School it is a regular feature. At home the parents must ensure its continuance. **Don't become Dady and mummy cool. Be their friend in need.**

Give them a feel of Adversity. Living with a facility may not be very helpful in life. The children must also be exposed to difficulties and adversities. The Residential School makes the students Rough and Tough. Too much protection may lead to low Self Esteem.

Bill Gates visited a restaurant for a cup of coffee. He gave a tip of five dollars to the waiter who served him. The waiter told him' sir yesterday your son was here and he gave a tip of twenty five dollars'. He is the son of a billionaire and I am the son of a carpenter.' Replied Bill Gates.

Criticize the Behavior not the Child. This is for both teachers and parents. Leveling them as poor, slow learners, naughty, arrogant, loser, failure is always harmful. Too much appreciative and over critical comments lowers the self-esteem of the child. Watch their actions, reactions, behavior, attitude and habits. Most parents still issue multiple instructions to girls when they venture out but when boys step out **'Bye have fun'** is the only instruction.

No Comparison with other siblings and friends. There are the instances when the children have taken extreme steps including suicide merely because of comparison with others particularly about Academic Performance. Treat your son and daughter as equal. **Boys will be boys' dictum** is now be done away with.

Parenting is a pure pleasure. Must feel overwhelmed by the responsibility of raising kids. Much preaching, talking about self-achievements, boasting, difficulties faced, hard work done etc. is taken as Generation Gap.

Develop Healthy Eating Habits in your Child. The students in Boarding School don't get any junk food. Fresh and nutritious food is served. The children may take some liberty at home. The parents must also serve them home cooked fresh food and avoid any fast or junk food. Make them feel your warmth and coolness.

Don't promise more than you can deliver but deliver more than you promise. Strike the right balance. A warm hug, an honest appreciation are more motivational than expensive gifts or speculative words.

Be positive to instil positiveness in your children. The parents leave both a tangible and intangible impact on their siblings. One negative thought can shatter thousands of dreams. **'One tree makes one lakh matchsticks but one matchstick can burn lacs of trees'.**

Never force your choices and Preferences on them. Let the children choose the stream and careers of their choices. The mindset of traditional Engineers and Doctors needs to be changed. Children are wise enough to decide their future course. Find a son or daughter in your child, not a professional.

Make Technology a Boon and not a Bane. In this era technology has become part of life. The information is abundant but may not be accurate. The children are over busy with digital gadgets even the parents. The parents need to mend their ways first and their children afterwards.

Be a Role Model for your Children. Child observes his/her parents very closely and picks up good as well as bad traits. Their gestures, postures, qualities, temperament, language used, habits etc. are picked up even before entering school. So the parents have to be very careful about all this. The best role model can be the parents.

The parents of the children studying in Residential School have to be vigilant when they come home. Little carelessness may adversely affect the values and good habits developed in school. Such an environment needs to be created so that the children find their school at home. If comprehend appropriately, the following Indian old saying is very relevant in the present scenario also

"पूत कपूत तो क्यो ंधन सचंय,
पूत सपूत तो क्यो ंधन सचंय।"

CHAPTER XX

Enthusiastic Students

"'If you want to bring any change in society,
begin with students'
Mahatma Gandhi "

Students are the most important stakeholders in any Educational Institution. In Fact the Personality of School is made or marred by the students. The traditions, culture, discipline and values developed in school fully depend on students. The school earns its name and fame because of the laurels brought by the students in various fields. Even after passing out from school, students shine in several professions making their Alma Mater proud.

Some Advantages.

Residential Schools provide ample opportunities to grow and develop. They mould and shape the personality of a child in such a manner that he/she succeeds in every endeavor of life.

Lays a strong foundation of discipline, virtues and character. Students become habitual of all this. Many students may not have excelled in exams but did exceedingly well in life.

Promote self-confidence, self-dependence and self-esteem. Top priority is accorded to Self-Development. All initiatives and programs of The Residential Schools provide self-development opportunities.

Being Residential, the Students are in school all the time. Hidden talents of students and their immense

potentials can be observed by their teachers and provide them development opportunities accordingly.

Excellence is both the vision and mission of Residential School. It is not only Academic excellence but strives to achieve excellence in every field. **Promoting brilliance, prioritizing EQ and physical well-being are the known characteristic features.**

Teaching morality, empathy and Social behavior. The students learn the greatest lessons of life. The schools teach them to see dreams not by closed eyes but open eyes. They become more thoughtful. They follow the moral code taught in school throughout their lives and become successful persons and responsible citizens. Teachers teach them how to use their imagination to build character and create their background.

These schools shape the young minds, drive innovation and create leaders for tomorrow.

Students feel inspired, supported and loved. This gives them a feel of being at home.

Some Tips For Students.

Students are fortunate enough to have come to a Residential School where there is tremendous scope for growth and development. School provides the best platform to become an all-rounder. But the best teachers, the best facilities and the best environment may not benefit them unless they are willing to learn and strive for excellence. **'Where there is a will there's a way'.**

There is no alternative to hard work, it never goes in vain.

'Arise, Awake and Stop not till the Goal is Achieved'.
Swami Vivekanand.

Students follow this ideology in Residential schools.

This is rather the era of SMART WORK. Must work smarty and wholeheartedly, good results will automatically come. Hard work results in making rapid strides in every sphere.

Competition with self. Residential School instills competitive zeal and spirit in students. Their competition is not with others but with self i.e. Doing **better than before.** Japanese people **succeed** because of their KAIZEN philosophy which means performing better.

Self Motivation.

"If mind can conceive, heart can believe, I can achieve"Mohammad Ali.

Be proud of your achievements and accomplishments. One can not be supported by external motivation from teachers and parents unless one feels motivated from within. **'Yes I have done it, I can do much better should be the call coming from within. Provide special impetus to self. Believe in your inner voice. Love thyself.**

Be Positive.

"Mind is our best friend but our worst enemy."
Churchill.

Think positive. Don't let negativity surround you. Be positive to self and others. One negative thought can badly damage our actions and behavior. Many may not excel in exams but did exceedingly well elsewhere. Never regret a day in your life. **Good days give you happiness, bad days give you experience, the worst days teach you lessons and the best days give you memories.** Positive thinking builds a high self-esteem. Positive feeling is pleasure.

Always remember

Road has a speed limit.

Bank has money. Limit.

But

Thinking has no limit.

So think big, dream big and achieve big.

Doing away with Examination Fever.

Most students suffer from examination fever. They lose their cool and become stressed. But Residential School has all kinds of support and guidance required for solid preparation. Teachers are always there to guide them, to clear their doubts and motivate them. So the students are the least scared of the examination. The students are therefore suggested to treat the exams ...

Not a fear but a festival...

celebrate it.

Not a threat but an opportunity...

avail it.

Not a problem but a solution....

enjoy it.

Not a trouble but a challenge..

accept it.

Not getting higher grades but higher learning...

understand it.

Students of Residential schools become exam proof as they are used to a number of exams, class test, unit test, diagnostic test, periodic test, terminal exams, term exams and others.

Learning by writing is the best style.

These days students lack writing speed. The reason is perhaps they are not exposed to learning by writing strategy. Slow speed results in less scoring because all the questions are not attempted. Whereas this is the best method to grasp and understand the content. It will improve the speed, spellings, sentence formation and handwriting. The students can score much better.

Make Excellence a Habit.

Residential School keeps the students gainfully busy in both scholastic and co scholastic activities. There are good avenues to excel. The students excel also. Most students make it a habit and this is a good habit.

Groom your Personality.

Our personality is our greatest asset. It is the combination of our thinking, behavior, actions, manners, character, our health.

Pleasing manners always make friends of foe, pungent manners ever make a friend to go. Values and virtues are not hereditary, they are learnt.

Communication Skills.

This is the era of commu*nication*. Good communication is one of the personality traits. In Residential Schools there is good scope for sharpening one's communication skills. Students need to improve their reading, writing, speaking and listening skills. Must come forward to participate in morning assembly activities, literary, cultural and scientific activities. Both verbal and non-verbal communication are equally important.

Those who can talk better will shine brighter.

Health is wealth. Good food, healthy life style, eating habits, physical exercise and sound sleep are the ingredients of good health. Fortunately, Residential School provides all this. Sound sleep is a luxury these days. In Residential School the schedule is so hectic that the students are gainfully busy every time, so enjoy sound and quality sleep. Such a culture of the school **Prevents illness, promote wellness.**

Help yourself.

Gandhiji was a great manager of human affairs. He never asked anybody to do what he didn't do himself.

Residential schools do not provide family like comforts and facilities. The students are taught to be self-dependent. They have to manage themselves in every affair.

Manage your Time.

Time is money. Those who have understood the value of time, easily climb the ladder of success. The schedule is so hectic that without effective time management one can neither be punctual nor disciplined. Particularly during exams, time is the main hurdle in scoring better. It is often noticed that due to improper time management, the students are unable to attempt the entire question paper, even if they know the answer, leaving some questions because of paucity of time. Time is always scarce and the time gone never comes back.

Be a fighter, never give up. A false start is better than no start. Residential School poses many challenges, face them with all your might.

Learn with happiness and excitement.

'Learning never exhausts the mind'.

Leonardo da Vinci

Learning is a lifelong process, there is no end at any stage of life. Be attentive in class, alert in the play field, effective in house and loveable among the teachers. Happiness is an inside job, it is a state of mind, it is priceless and more of all, it is free. It is the best immunity booster. **Judge everything** you will be happy, forgive **everything you will be happier, love everything you will be happiest.**

The role of students in every society is vital. We can see our future leaders, bureaucrats, professionals and citizens in them. Moreover, the young ones are easily influenced and inspired. **Only young bamboo can be bent, if you try to bend the old one, it will break.**

CHAPTER XXI

Types of Residential Schools

Residential School is a centuries old concept. As discussed earlier, The Gurukuls in ancient times provided residential education. There are instances of this system in vedic period focusing on Shrawan (Listening) Chintan and Manan (thinking, reflection) Now different categories of Residential Schools have emerged all over the world. A good number of Residential Schools are run by the central and state govts. There are innumerable Residential Schools run by the different educational groups. Approximately the number of Residential Schools in both public and private sectors is more than 45000 in India. More than 65 education boards are there to grant affiliation such as CBSE, ICSE, IB and state boards.

There are different types of Boarding Schools functioning in India and abroad. Some of them can be categorised as

1. **Residential Schools run by the central and state govts.**
2. **Residential Schools run by trusts, missions.**
3. **Privately owned Residential Schools.**
4. **Exclusively boys Boarding Schools.**
5. **Exclusively Girls Boarding Schools.**
6. **Co Educational Boarding Schools.**

At present the following types of Residential schools are functioning in our country.

Exclusively Residential Schools

These schools are in both public and private sectors. Most of them are coeducational. However, there are schools only for boys as well as only for girls.

Govt sector Schools:

Jawahar Navodaya Vidyalayas

These Schools came into existence in 1986. The education policy of 1985 emphasized on opening residential schools in rural areas to provide quality education to the talented children. These schools are from classes six to twelve, affiliated with CBSE. JNVs are now in almost all the districts of India except the state of Tamil Nadu. These are fully funded by the govt of India. Schools are known for quality results, values, holistic personality development and very successful alumnus. At present there are about 660 JNVs.

Central Tibetan Schools

The govt. of India founded the Central Tibetan Schools Administration to take the responsibility of educating the Tibetan refugees in 1961. Until 2022 67 such schools were run by CTSA all over India in Tibetan settlements. The schools are residential and coeducational. These are fully funded by the government. But in 2022 the govt. handed over these schools to the Central Tibetan Administration.

Eklavya Model Residential Schools

These schools were started by the Ministry of Tribal Affairs in the year 1997-98 in tribal areas. These are also coeducational schools from six to twelve and fully funded by the govt of India. These are specifically meant for SC/ST categories. At present there are about 690 schools and more are likely to come up.

Rajiv Gandhi Navodaya Vidyalayas

These are also Residential Coeducational Schools run by the govt of Uttarakhand on the lines of JNVs. This is also a district scheme and out of 13 districts there are eight Rajiv Navodaya Vidyalayas. First Rajiv Gandhi Navodaya Vidyalaya was set up in 2003.

Atal Avasiya Vidyalayas

The UP government started these schools in the year 2023. These are for the children of construction workers. At present 18 such schools are functional in UP.

Rashtriya Military Schools

These are exclusively for boys. The first Military School was started in1922 at Chail in Himachal Predesh. There are five Military Schools in India. The primary objective is to prepare the children for armed forces. The schools are fully funded by the Ministry of Defence.

Sainik Schools

These schools are run by the Sainik Schools Society under the ministry of defence. First school came into being in 1961. The number of Sainik Schools is 33. These were boys schools but now the entry of girls has also been allowed. 33 percent seats are reserved for girls. The objective is almost similar as of Military Schools.

Rashtriya Indian Military College (RIMC)

This is the only college of its kind in Dehradun. Before 1947 it was known as **Prince Wales Royal Indian Military School**. The college was formerly exclusively for boys.

Asharam Schools

The govt has started some 850 such schools in the States of Andhra Pradesh, Karnataka, Tamil Nadu and Gujarat. These Schools provide free Residential Education to the Tribal Children. The schools are up to Secondary level.

Kasturba Gandhi Avaseeya Balika Vidyalayas

The Govt. of India started this scheme in the year 2004 under Sarva Shiksha Abhiyan. This is Block level scheme exclusively for girls belonging to SC, ST, OBC and minority communities. The govt has proposed to set up these residential schools for girls in almost all the blocks in the majority of districts. At present more than 3700 KGABVs are functional.

Private Residential Schools:

Missionary Schools

These schools are the oldest Residential Schools run by the Christian Missionaries particularly by the Catholic Church. Some of them started in 18th century. They are known for their academic standard and traditions. Initially their objective was the spread of English Education and conversion. There are more than 13000 Missionary Schools in India. Most of them have earned good name and fame and therefore, admission in these schools is difficult. The popular Schools belong to St. Thomas, St. George's, St. Joseph, St. Marries, St. Jude's etc.

Acharayakulam

Yoga Guru Swami Ramdev has come forward with innovative ideas of providing Residential Quality Education having components of both Vedic And Modern Education. These schools are known as Avharayakulam. Swami ji has proposed to set up about six hundred such schools in India and overseas. At present there are two Acharayakulam in Haridwar and Ranchi. These are English Medium Schools from classes VI to XII.

Elite Private Residential Schools:

The Doon School, Dehradun

This is one of the finest public schools in Dehradun. Founded in 1935 the school is known for its quality education and wonderful traditions. It is the most expensive school for Boys. Many celebrities are the Alumni of the School.

Mayo College, Ajmer

This is also a boys school set up in 1875. The school was set for the wards of Royal Families.

The Scindia School, Gwalior

Founded in 1897, also for the Royals and Nobles. It is also a boys School. The school is known for its state of art facilities and high standards.

The Lawrence School, Sanawar

The school came into being in the year 1847 in the hills of Solan Himachal Predesh. This is a coeducational School.

The Woodstock School

It is one of the oldest Residential Schools in Mussoorie. It was started in 1854. Most of the students are from abroad.

Welham Girls School

This exclusively girls school started in the year 1957 in Dehradun. The school has classes from VI to XII.

The Rishi Valley School

The school is situated in Chittoor, Andhra Pradesh. The school follows the ideology and Philosophy of Eminem educationist and Philosopher JK Krishnamurthy.

Sherwood College

The school is located in green and serene surroundings of Nainital. It came into existence in the year 1869. It is coeducational and affiliated to ICSE and International Boards.

Many other influential and known boarding schools include Kodaikanal International School, The Lawrence School Ooty, St. Paul Kolkata, Sai Institute of Educare Chennai, GD Goenka World School, Delhi, Swaminarayan Gurukul, Hyderabad Vibgyor High School Pune etc.

Most of the elite boarding schools are located in famous hill stations, Mussoorie, Darjeeling, Nainital, Shimla, Nilgiri Hills etc. The reason behind is the suitable climate, free from pollution, peaceful environment and green surroundings.

Besides, a good number of schools are run by Ramakrishna Mission, DAV trust and other charitable and Philanthropic Organisations.

About The Author

R P Dobhal started his teaching career from an eminent Residential School in Mussoorie. He spent more than 35 years in Residential Schools in different capacities as a teacher, Principal, Educational Administration And a Trainer. He retired from Navodaya Vidyalaya Samiti as an Assistant Commissioner. He has subscribed a number of articles about Pedagogical Concerns to several Newspapers and Magazines. This is the fourth book written by him. The previous three are

1. A Guide to Effective Teaching
2. Principal with Principles
3. Raju Bechara(Hindi Autobiography)

And the latest is the fourth, 'Residential School A Home Away From Home'. The author has made an attempt to deal with all those areas of a Boarding school which need the attention of Principals, Teachers, Parents, Students and management. He began his career as a professional from a Residential School and superannuated from the most prestigious Residential Schools System.

Connect With The Author

Youtube : <u>RPD Academics</u>

www.youtube.com/c/rpdacademics

RPD Academics is an educational channel that aims to promote effective teaching. Teaching is done but effective teaching is rare. RPD Academics aims to increase the number of effective teachers. Videos that provide effective teaching startegies are uploaded here.

FaceBook : <u>rajendraprasad.dobhal</u>

www.facebook.com/rajendraprasad.dobhal

Email : <u>rpdobhal@gmail.com</u>